SAINT–JUST: APOSTLE OF THE TERROR

SAINT-JUST
APOSTLE OF THE TERROR

BY
GEOFFREY BRUUN

ARCHON BOOKS
HAMDEN CONNECTICUT
1966

TO
I. M. B.
AND
E. T. B.

CONTENTS

FOREWORD TO THE 1966 EDITION

AT THE TIME I wrote this biography of Saint-Just I had immersed myself for several years in the study of his career and character. There was scarcely a line of his speeches or writings that I could not have recognized at sight, and I then possessed a day-to-day familiarity with his thoughts and actions that has since lost its intimacy and defies recapture.

This realization has stayed my hand whenever I contemplated rewriting a page or revising an opinion before the biography was reissued. It seemed to me that whatever virtues the book may claim depend upon an insight, I might almost say an identification, that once united me with my subject. Even the terse prose of the narrative, the laconic sentences, are echoes of Saint-Just's style and personality. But they are echoes to which I have ceased to vibrate and to which I cannot reattune my ear.

There is a second reason for letting the study remain as originally written. Although several books on Saint-Just have subsequently appeared (they are listed on page 163) none of them has led me to reverse my judgments on his career or personality. Nor has any neglected source material come to my attention that contradicts that career as I reconstructed it when I was nearer Saint-Just's age and nearer to understanding him.

Ithaca, New York
October 20, 1965   GEOFFREY BRUUN

SAINT-JUST:
APOSTLE OF THE TERROR

. .

INTRODUCTION

In the gallery of *arrivistes* who were swept into prominence
by the French Revolution, there is no figure more sharply
etched, and at the same time more enigmatic, than that of
Louis Antoine de Saint-Just. He came to Paris in September, 1792, as a deputy of the National Convention, and
almost immediately he leaped to fame. Within ten
months, at the age of twenty-five, he was a member of the
Committee of Public Safety, one of those terrible decemvirs whose prodigious energy saved the Revolution.
Within two years he was dead. On those whom he encountered during that swift passage he left an impression
so vivid that they sought in vain for phrases trenchant
enough to describe him. 'The apocalyptic Saint-Just,'
Courtois called him.[1] 'A brain of fire, a heart of ice,' was
Barère's famous summary.[2] 'One of the most despotic
heads in the Convention,' declared the judicial Lindet.
'A youth cold, ferocious, and sanguinary.'[3] 'His enthusiasm,' affirmed Levasseur, 'was born of a mathemati-
cal certainty.... To found the Republic of his dreams he
would have given his head, and a hundred thousand heads
with it.'[4] This implacability of character was reflected in
his face. 'He had regular features,' wrote one who had
seen him often, 'a scornful glance, and an austere expression. His air, in general, was one of anxiety, a sort of

---

[1] E. B. Courtois, *Rapport fait... le 16 nivôse an III*, p. 26.
[2] Bertrand Barère de Vieuzac, *Mémoires* (4 vols., Paris, 1842), I, 235.
[3] Armand Montier, *Robert Lindet* (Paris, 1899), p. 249.
[4] René Levasseur, *Mémoires* (4 vols., Paris, 1879), II, 324.

gloomy and concentrated defiance, and his tone and manner were utterly frigid. Such was our impression of Saint-Just, a youth not yet thirty years old.' [1]

It is remarkable that Saint-Just's rôle in the Revolution should so often have been dismissed as that of a mere lieutenant of Robespierre. More energetic than Robespierre, and more ruthless, he shared of his own right in every major revolutionary crisis from September, 1792, to July, 1794. He was active in the trial of the king; he helped to draft the Constitution of 1793; and he entered the Committee of Public Safety ahead of Robespierre himself. As spokesman for the Committee he won a succession of brilliant victories over the Convention, and it fell to his lot to read the indictments which sent Hébert and Danton to the guillotine. Yet these parliamentary triumphs represent only one phase of his work. Half his time was spent with the republican armies, where he participated, in Alsace and on the Sambre, in the decisive campaigns of the Year II.

To trace, therefore, the twenty-two months of Saint-Just's public career is to reconstruct the history of the Revolution during its most dynamic period. But his significance runs deeper than a chance contact with critical events. Better than any of his colleagues on the Committee of Public Safety, Saint-Just exemplifies the ideas leavening the social upheaval. His education, his ambition, the whole bent of his mind fitted him to become an apostle of the revolutionary faith. 'I feel within me,' he averred, 'something which triumphs with the age.' [2] Thus, while a study of his services, political and military, illuminates the tense struggle of 1793 and 1794, a study of

[1] M. P. Paganel, *Essai historique et critique sur la Révolution française* (Paris, ˘810), p. 238. Quoted in *Annales historiques de la Révolution française*, IV (1913), 3. ˘.

[2] *Œuvres complètes de Saint-Just*, edited by Charles Vellay (2 vols., Paris, 1908), I, 349. This work is cited hereafter under the abbreviation O.C.

his philosophy does more. In Saint-Just's writings may be found, in their most lucid and laconic form, the tenets of the revolutionary creed. The progress of his thought is a spiritual history of the Revolution.

The ease with which he assimilated the dominant ideas of the age brought to Saint-Just the conviction that he was in league with elemental forces. 'Because I am young,' he wrote, 'I think that I am closer to Nature.'[1] It was this inward assurance that he was a herald from the future, and that the stars in their courses would fight on his side, that invested his phrases with their thrilling certitude, and lent him the air which Courtois termed *apocalyptic*. The sensations of doubt, hesitation or remorse, which confused others, seemed powerless to trouble his implacable resolve. 'I have left all weakness behind,' he boasted. 'I have seen in the universe nothing but the truth, and I have proclaimed it.'[2]

He was too young to learn tolerance for others, too successful to harbour doubts of himself, and too lacking in humour to suspect that he might be clinging to a pose instead of a principle. Placing his feet unequivocally upon what appeared to be the predestined road, he moved forward with a defiant step, intrepid and austere. If it was a pose, at least he preserved it faithfully until the knife of the guillotine flickered above him in the light of the setting sun.

[1] O.C., I, 252.   [2] O.C., II, 494.

CHAPTER I
AN ILL BEGINNING

J'ai vingt ans; j'ai mal fait; je pourrai faire mieux.
SAINT-JUST, Preface to *Organt*.[1]

To THE little village of Blérancourt, in Picardy, there came to live in 1776 a retired French army officer with his wife and three young children. Jean de Saint-Just de Riche-bourg, as he styled himself, was not of noble birth, a fact which helps to explain why thirty years of service under Louis XV had brought him the Cross of Saint Louis, but no higher rank than that of captain of cavalry. A disappointed man, he threw up his commission in 1767, and married Jeanne Marie Robinot, the daughter of a notary of Decize, in the Nivernais. There a son was born to him the following year, and baptized Louis Antoine.[2] From 1768 to 1776 the retired captain acted as manager on the estate of a Monsieur de Buat, Seigneur de Morsain, in Picardy; but in the latter year he moved to Blérancourt, where he had purchased a comfortable house and garden on the outskirts of the town. He planned to pass a restful old age amid the semi-pastoral surroundings, but his dream was cut short by death the following year.

Madame de Saint-Just, left a widow with three young children in a town many leagues from her birthplace, devoted herself wholly to their care and education. To save a *dot* of twenty thousand francs for each of her daughters, and establish her son Antoine in a respectable profession, became her life's purpose, and to accomplish it she was willing to sacrifice leisure and luxury. It seemed to her a harsh reward for such devotion to have her son grow

[1] O.C., I, 2.
[2] The record of the birth and baptism of Louis Antoine de Saint-Just de Richebourg is preserved at the Mairie, Decize, Département de la Nièvre.

yearly more arrogant in spirit and more ungrateful. The Oratorian Monks, to whom she entrusted Antoine's education,[1] quickened his mind without curbing his imperious temper. When he returned home from their college at Soissons in his eighteenth year, Madame de Saint-Just felt the full weight of her responsibility. A profession had to be found for her son. The Church, she knew, would never suit him; but the law offered a creditable alternative whereby he might rise in time to an honoured place in the community. To secure him the benefit of apprenticeship with a reputable notary she was prepared to meet the necessary fees.

This sensible and worthy plan seemed destined to be wrecked by her son's intractability. His ambition, at eighteen, was to win fame with either sword or pen, but his mother opposed both careers, feeling, perhaps, that the first might prove dangerous and the second disreputable. As the summer of 1786 drew towards autumn, and the peasants of Picardy gathered in the harvest, the Saint-Just home in the little village of Blérancourt became the scene of bitter arguments. Antoine's contempt for provincial dullness, and his avid dreams of the great world of Paris, hurt his mother deeply and alarmed her more. He was her only son, and she could see him growing daily more alien and uncontrollable. Perhaps it was instinct as much as reason which drove her to clutch more firmly the one hold over him which remained at her command. She tightened the purse strings.

A letter to the Chevalier d'Evry, an old friend of the Saint-Justs living in Paris, tells the result.

I am in the greatest distress [Madame de Saint-Just wrote on September 17, 1786], and I am hoping that you will lessen it by doing me a favour. My son has been staying with me for some

[1] Maurice Dommanget, 'La famille de Saint-Just,' *Annales révolutionnaires*, VI (1913), 517-21.

weeks, and last Friday night he left for Paris without my knowledge, taking with him a new silver bowl marked with an E and an R; a silver goblet with the base embossed, engraved with the name St.-Just; a cup of half bottle measure, the base and rim inlaid with gold, marked with the name of Robinot, vicar of Decize; three heavy silver cups; a bundle of silver braid; a pair of pistols with gold inlay work; a narrow ring set with a rose stone; and several other small things of silver, all of which he appropriated without my knowledge. His plan, most probably, is to dispose of them, and thus procure money for some wrongful purpose or other. Such conduct has hurt me deeply, and as it is a matter of concern to me to attempt the recovery of all these trinkets, and to guard against and check the course of my son's misconduct, I will be indebted to you, Sir, if you will go to the trouble of visiting the police authorities, and securing an order from them that an immediate search be made for my son, so that he may be forced to return the property he has taken, and then secured in some place where he will no longer be exposed to such temptation, and will have time to repent his error....

Sir, your humble and very obedient servant,

ROBINOT, widow of St.-Just.[1]

The decision to punish her son with imprisonment must have cost Madame de Saint-Just the deepest pain, but she clung to it with admirable firmness. A few days after his flight she received an indirect communication from the fugitive, and her treatment of it is eloquent of her outraged feelings. The letter was written by a self-styled doctor of medicine, who signed himself Richardet, and informed Madame de Saint-Just that her son had been suffering from an obscure but serious ailment. This, the doctor was happy to assure her, had yielded to his treatments; but he was grieved to learn that the young man, in order to discharge his medical expenses, had disposed of some of the family silver. The boy, he added, was staying

[1] Charles Vatel, *Charlotte de Corday et les Girondins* (3 vols., Paris, 1864–72), I, Préface, cxli-cxlii.

in Paris, at the Hôtel Saint Louis, too proud and sensitive to return home; and the doctor urged Madame de Saint-Just to write him a conciliatory letter, since otherwise he might continue his wandering. Madame was not deceived. She sent the doctor's missive to Paris, to D'Evry, with the comment that she did not believe a word of it, that her son had been in excellent health, and the whole letter appeared to her a trick designed to excite her anxiety and pave the way to forgiveness for the prodigal.

If the letter was indeed a product of Saint-Just's pen, or at least of his connivance, it proved a tactical error on his part, for it betrayed his hiding-place to D'Evry and to the police. He was arrested September 30, and placed in the custody of Dame Marie de Saint Colombe at Picpus, in a house of correction to which children of good family were sent for disciplinary purposes. Madame de Saint-Just's expressed determination to check the course of her son's misconduct was evidently no idle threat.

On October 6 the police interrogated their prisoner. He declared under oath that he was named Louis Antoine de Saint-Just, that he had neither title nor profession, was nineteen years of age, and a native of Decize in the Nivernais. His place of residence he gave as Blérancourt in Picardy, at the home of his mother, but he explained that recently he had been registered at the Hôtel Saint Louis, rue Fromenteau. To the questions, why and when he had left Blérancourt, he replied that he had left some five weeks earlier because his mother had sent him to Paris. As it was then three weeks to a day since his nocturnal departure, this misrepresentation of the time and motive of his journey suggests that Saint-Just still hoped that the police were acting without definite evidence against him. The next question undeceived him. Asked categorically whether he had taken with him some of his mother's silver, he admitted the theft frankly, and explained that he had sold the property later in Paris.

He was accordingly returned to his prison, and on October 15 an application was forwarded to the Baron de Breteuil, Secretary of State and Minister of the Royal Household, to authorize the arrest of the 'S^r de St Just' and his confinement in the house of Dame Marie at his mother's pleasure and expense.[1]

No formal charge was lodged against him. The *Régistre de la Préfecture de Police* does not mention a term for his imprisonment and records only that he was held 'at the demand of his mother.' Saint-Just himself accepted his fate with cool disdain; and as the days passed his mother realized with increasing bitterness that the severity to which she had steeled herself could wear a double edge. 'I will decide from his subsequent deportment whether he deserves my affection sufficiently for me to let him leave his retreat,'[2] she wrote D'Evry October 18; but the prisoner maintained a stubborn and contemptuous silence. Madame de Saint-Just's health began to fail beneath the strain imposed by this battle of wills. 'I wish him to show some sign of regret for the grief he has caused me,' she wrote again November 7. 'If he has a spark of affection left, he ought to upbraid himself for the sorrow he has brought me, which might well have killed me in my state of health. It is a wicked return for the tenderness and affection which I have always lavished upon him.'[3]

The prisoner remained unmoved by these reproaches: it would be, perhaps, an unkindness to suggest that he was inured to them. His captivity, while irksome, was not proving insupportable, for he was well treated and had the resources of an active mind to draw upon. 'One must hope,' Madame de Saint-Just had confided to D'Evry, '... that, realizing his errors, he will employ his thoughts in planning how to make me some atonement and provide

---

[1] Vatel, *op. cit.*, I, Préface, cxlviii; Antoine Morsain, 'Quelques antécédents de Saint-Just,' *Mercure de France*, LVX (1907), 201.

[2] Morsain, *op. cit.*, p. 203.   [3] *Ibid.*, p. 204.

himself with a respectable occupation.'[1] It was a pious wish but it proved how little she understood her son's character. Saint-Just preferred to follow the devices and desires of his own heart, and was passing the hours of his enforced leisure pleasantly enough in the composition of a long epic poem. This fruit of a winter's idleness, published two years later under the title *Organt*, reflects the young poet in a wide variety of moods, but repentance is not one of them. A passage such as the following, wherein Satan addresses his fallen compeers, offers an ironic commentary on the faith Madame de Saint-Just had expressed in the chastening influences of solitude.

> De mon forfait, je n'ai point de remord;
> Par un nouveau couronnons notre audace,
> Et vengeons-nous de l'injure du sort.
> Il l'a voulu; par un coup de tonnerre
> Précipités du séjour de lumière,
> Le noir Ténare, en ses flancs odieux,
> Servit d'asile à l'élite des Dieux.
> J'ai tout perdu, ma dignité suprême,
> Mon sceptre d'or, et ce trône immortel
> Qui dominait les Puissances du Ciel;
> Mais, malgre tout, je suis encor moi-même,
> Indépendant des arrêts du Destin,
> J'étais un Dieu, je le serai sans fin....[2]

This dreary epic of eight thousand lines, Saint-Just's first literary effort to reach print, has so little to distinguish it beyond its length that further quotations are superfluous. With eighteenth-century frankness, unrelieved by any charm, it relates the wars, amours and stratagems of a motley throng of gods and mortals. The characters which crowd it are pillaged at random from mythology, history and theology, and swept together in a stream of verse remarkable chiefly for its echoing plagiarisms. Heroines

[1] Morsain, *op. cit.*, p. 202.   [2] O.C., I, 23.

are abducted and rescued, paladins clash in battle, the
gods of Olympus and the Christian hierarchy applaud the
human comedy, and choruses of nymphs seduce the un-
wary voyager. It would appear that the author himself
appreciated the fantastic incoherence of the work, for he
appended as preface the quotation: *Vous, jeune homme, au
bon sens avez vous dit adieu.*[1]

Nevertheless, despite its license and its artificiality,
Organt reveals in Saint-Just a feeling for the impact of
words and a gift for compelling phrases. The metrical
facility is surprising, and the onrush of ideas and images almost conceals at times the total lack of inspiration. There
is satire without humour, and sentiment without sincerity. The poet never mines his own ore, never speaks in
his proper person; his figures, scenes and episodes all have
the disquieting effect of familiar pictures in a foreign
frame. Those idle hours at Picpus gave Saint-Just an opportunity to pour into fluent verse all the borrowings of a
precocious immaturity; but the result was not a poem, it
was a long exercise in rhetoric.

So the winter passed, while Madame de Saint-Just
awaited in vain the apology which she had demanded from
her son as the price of his release. By February the worry
had brought her to her bed, but bodily infirmities could not
shake her will. She requested D'Evry to inform her son
that if he made amends and promised to take up the study
of law, a position as solicitor's clerk was open to him in
Soissons, but that he would be released on no other con-
ditions. Being a man of tact, D'Evry apparently re-
drafted this ultimatum in more persuasive terms, ad-
dressing the prisoner as one man of the world to another,
and urging acceptance. Still Saint-Just hesitated, determined not to quit his citadel without the honours of war.

---

[1] O.C., I, 1. The line is quoted without acknowledgment from the 'Satire du
XVIII siècle' by Nicolas-Joseph-Laurent Gilbert. See Gilbert's *Œuvres*, edited
by Charles Nodier (Paris, 1840), p. 26.

Two weeks passed before he replied, and his letter, when composed, was a masterpiece of dignified capitulation.

Allow me to offer you a thousand apologies [he wrote D'Evry February 26] for my failure to answer before this the letter which you did me the honour of writing me. A fever which attacked me two weeks ago made it impossible for me to hold a pen; but it proved to be nothing serious, and I am once more in good health.

I am deeply obliged to you, Sir, for the advice you offer. I shall adhere to it, unless I abandon a course I had already set myself, for a resolution to mend my ways anticipated your persuasions. I have written Mother, enclosing to her a letter for Rigaux. I am counting upon the success of that application unless I have already been forestalled by others. You suggested in your letter that it would be fitting to direct my reply to Mother in order that she might send it on; this was precisely my intention, since I have no great desire to make known to him my present address. But I thank you none the less, Sir, for making the suggestion, for where my act was perhaps one of self-interest, you have made it seem a gesture of propriety. This proves, Sir, that your perception is much keener and more delicate than mine. To even the score I can only assure you of the depth of my esteem and gratitude, for these are sentiments which do not depend on keenness of wit.

I have the honour to be, Sir, your very humble and very obedient servant,

DE SAINT-JUST [1]

This resolution to mend his ways did not win Saint-Just his freedom; he had to supplement it with expressions of regret for his mother's suffering. 'Maman, it appears, is growing steadily worse,' he conceded to D'Evry. 'It is a grief to me, for I cannot hide from myself that I am partly responsible for her illness, through the anxiety which I have caused her. But it is impossible to return to the past;

[1] Ernest Hamel, 'Une épisode de la jeunesse de Saint-Just,' *La Révolution française*, XXXII (1897), 115.

the only remedy in my power is the future.'[1] Madame de Saint-Just was not yet appeased, and refused to have any direct communication with her son, but she consented to let D'Evry release him and bring him back to Blérancourt. Of the prodigal's welcome home, at the end of March, there is no record, but it cannot have been prolonged, for he took up his duties almost immediately as clerk to a Monsieur Dubois Descharmes in Soissons. Her mind relieved by this happy solution to the struggle, Madame de Saint-Just was apparently able to regain her health, for she lived to be seventy-six.

In Soissons, Saint-Just formed friendships which endured through later years, but of his actual life there nothing has survived save legends. He forsook the city in September, 1787, to register at the School of Law in Rheims, where, having passed an entrance examination on the 24th of that month, he became a candidate for the baccalaureate degree. This he gained on February 14, 1788, and four weeks later he was awarded his *licence ès lois*. Unfortunately, of his life in Rheims, as in Soissons, almost nothing is known, a fact the more to be regretted because the *Faculté de Droit* there trained many who were later leaders in the Revolution, including Brissot, Condorcet, Couthon, Danton and Prieur (de la Marne). But it is improbable that Saint-Just met any of these men there in 1787, for they had all graduated before his time. On the other hand, he must almost certainly have come to know Jean Louis Deville, his future colleague in the National Convention, for he spent the winter in the same house as Deville, at No. 4, rue des Anglais. In honour of that sojourn the street has been called, since 1903, the rue Saint-Just.[2]

[1] Alfred Bégis, *Curiosités révolutionnaires. Saint-Just, membre du comité de salut public de la Convention nationale, 1767–1794. Son emprisonnement sous Louis XVI en exécution d'une lettre de cachet* (Paris, 1892), p. 32.

[2] Gustave Laurent, 'Le Faculté de Droit de Reims et les hommes de la Révolution,' *Annales historiques de la Révolution française*, XVII (1929), 329–58.

The successes which her son had gained in his legal studies can scarcely have failed to soften Madame de Saint-Just's heart when he returned to her in 1788. Her need of his presence and affection was keener than ever, for her two daughters were soon to marry and move away. To see him turn his attention to village affairs must have been balm to her spirit, and she provided funds for the expenses of his practice and for the purchase of some local property. One may hope that she enjoyed then a year or two of quiet happiness planning the future according to her desires, all unaware, like the rest of France, of the impending storm. She could not know that the city which had lured her son away from her once was preparing to call again, and that this time it would not give him back.

CHAPTER II
THE SLAVE OF ADOLESCENCE

O Dieu! faut-il que Brutus languisse oublié loin de Rome!
Saint-Just, Letter to Daubigny, July 20, 1792.[1]

Saint-Just's activities in the years between 1788 and 1792 would prove interesting without doubt, were a detailed reconstruction of them possible. But this chapter of his life, long a total blank to investigators, remains even today relatively incomplete. Nor is there much reason to hope that the picture can ever be filled in. A dozen letters, a handful of facts, is all that has rewarded a century of probing, and these are meagre sources from which to piece together an account of his life during four eventful years.

His residence throughout this period apparently continued to be his mother's house in Blérancourt, although he forsook it now and then for short excursions to the neighbouring cities of Chauny, Noyon and Soissons, and on at least two occasions he travelled as far as Paris. The first of these Parisian journeys occurred in the fateful summer of 1789. His nominal purpose in seeking the capital was to find a publisher for *Organt*, but the turbulent spectacle of history in the making soon turned his thoughts from literature to politics. Paris had become a stage for the rapidly unfolding drama of the Revolution, and all France was the audience. Saint-Just hastened from one point of interest to another, listened to the debates of the National Assembly, mingled with the crowds in the gardens of the Palais Royal, and cheered the National Guard. In some fashion, perhaps because they both hailed from the Noyonnais, he made the acquaintance of Camille Desmoulins, then a fiery young journalist in his twenties, who

[1] O.C., I, 348-49.

was already an idol of the populace. Saint-Just felt that he was breaking into charmed circles. He tried to assume the self-important air of the young revolutionaries whom he met, catch their shibboleths, and hint like them of conspiracies and threats. The clamour of a riot drew him to the spot with irresistible fascination, and he saw for the first time the unleashed fury of the mob in action, the reddened weapons, the distorted faces, the heads swept along on pikes.[1] But despite the attractions of Paris, he could not stay. With bitter reluctance he turned his back upon the tumult and the shouting and sought again the provincial dullness of Blérancourt.

His destiny had grown clear to him. Politics was the vocation he had been waiting to find; he would return to Paris after the next election as a representative of the people. Concealing his contempt for the silliness of local affairs, he defended his municipality in a suit with the Seigneur de Grenet over the title to some public lands, and he accepted a commission in the Blérancourt company of National Guards. Local politics were a ladder that could lift him from obscurity; his first emergence came in April, 1790, when he was despatched to Chauny to attend a conference held to decide between Laon and Soissons as a capital for the new Department of the Aisne. His speech on this occasion, the first recorded sample of his eloquence, was a defense of Soissons, on the ground that the poorer classes there were in desperate need and would benefit if the choice fell upon their city.

'Do not forget, gentlemen,' he begged, summing up his plea, 'how precious minutes are to the poor. Each of us ought to have come here with his opinion already formed, for while we deliberate, the children of some of our colleagues now present may be in want of bread, and be begging it from their weeping mothers. I cast my vote for Soissons.'[2] At heart Saint-Just cared little for the claims

[1] O.C., I, 257.   [2] O.C., I, 219.

of either city, and his pity for the poor was probably more
convenient than sincere. Yet he spoke with a show of
fervour that won applause. 'I mounted the tribune,' he
wrote Desmoulins, describing the incident, 'I tried to
swing the decision on the choice of a capital, but I failed
None the less, I departed laden with praise like an ass with
relics, confident that in the next legislature I may be with
you in the National Assembly.'[1]

Like all the young idealists of his day who had been
raised on the classics, Saint-Just professed unlimited admiration for the heroes of republican Rome. He affected
the laconic style, the Stoic faith, and the ruthless patriotism of a Brutus or a Cato. 'The world is empty since the
Romans went,' he lamented; and the conviction that
history could never recapture the grandeur that was
Rome, could never again produce in a degenerate age men
of the antique mould, seemed to him a fate too dark to
contemplate — 'the pity of it,' he wrote, 'tears my heart
and inhibits my pen.'[2] But there were others ready to
persuade him that in the ferment of the Revolution he
would see a renascence of all the ancient virtues, and
among these hopeful spirits was his new friend Camille
Desmoulins. 'Did you divine,' Camille had written his
father in the ardour of those early days, 'did you foresee,
when you baptized me Lucius Sulpicius Camillus that I
was to be a Roman?'[3]

To this reverence for the classical example Saint-Just
paid many a histrionic tribute, and a brilliant act which he
improvised in May, 1790, brought his name to the attention of the National Assembly. A pamphlet had been circulated in his Department, criticizing the Assembly for its
confiscation of the property of the Church.[4] Copies found

[1] O.C., I, 220-21. [2] O.C., I, 333.

[3] Camille Desmoulins, *Œuvres* (2 vols., Paris, 1836), II, 47.

[4] The pamphlet was entitled *Déclaration d'une partie de l'Assemblée Nationale sur un décret rendu le 16 avril, 1790, concernant la religion.*

their way into Saint-Just's hands, and he promptly denounced the brochure before the Municipal Council as a piece of counter-revolutionary propaganda. 'The whole Council,' the minutes of the meeting record, 'justly revolted by the abominable principles which the enemies of the Revolution were seeking to spread among the people, decreed: That the Declaration should be torn in pieces and burned forthwith, which being done on the spot, M. de Saint-Just, his hand over the flame of the libel, swore an oath to die for the fatherland, [and] the National Assembly, and to perish by fire like the pamphlet he had received rather than forget his vow. These words drew tears from all eyes.' [1] The members of the Council repeated the oath, and the president, in congratulating the young Scaevola, prophesied a brilliant career for him. Through his friendship with one Thullier, secretary to the Municipality, Saint-Just was able to make sure that a report of the incident went forward to Paris, and had the pleasure a few days later of reading the account in the records of the National Assembly.

July, 1790, found him once more in Paris, as head of a delegation of the Blérancourt National Guard sent there to participate in the *Fête de la Fédération*. If he visited the Assembly on this occasion, he may have heard Robespierre, as secretary, read the Report on Mendicity, and have been stirred by the deputies' paternal interest in the fate of the poor. This is surmise, but if true it would help to explain the curious letter which he despatched to Robespierre on his return to Blérancourt.

Blérancourt, by Noyon, August 19, 1790

You who sustain the Fatherland which is staggering under the flood of despotism and of intrigue [the flattery must have pleased the virtuous deputy from Arras, whose merit the Constituent Assembly had been so slow to recognize] you whom I know only

[1] *Archives parlementaires*, XV, 577.

as one knows God, by miracles, I address myself to you, Sir, to pray your assistance in saving my unfortunate district. The town of Courci has annexed to itself (so the report runs) the free markets of the borough of Blérancourt. Why do the cities swallow up the privileges of the countryside? Nothing remains to the latter except the taxes and imposts! Support, I beg you, with all your talent, a petition which I have sent by the same courier, in which I request the union of my patrimony with the national domains of the Canton, in order that my district may retain a privilege without which it must perish of famine. I do not know you, but you are a great man. You are not merely the deputy of a province, but of humanity and of the Republic. Act, I pray you, so that my petition may not be disregarded.

SAINT-JUST [1]

This generous disposal of a patrimony not yet in his possession was never carried through, and the gesture was designed, it would seem, merely to impress Robespierre and the electors of Blérancourt. Robespierre's vanity was touched, he kept the letter, and it formed the first link in a friendship that bound Saint-Just to him in life and death. Fortune was smiling on Saint-Just's campaign, and he decided to consolidate his reputation by placing before the public a statement of his views. His poem *Organt* had been published anonymously in 1789, and had been awarded a brief comment in Desmoulin's journal *Les Révolutions de France et de Brabant*. [2] But a political allegory which he wove in, with the idea of stimulating public interest, earned the displeasure of the authorities and the work was suppressed. [3] The second hostage which he now offered to fame fared more fortunately. Published in 1791 under

[1] O.C., I, 224.

[2] *Organt* was published towards the close of 1789, and advertised in the sixth number of Desmoulin's journal as follows: '*Organt*, Poëme en vingt chants, avec cette Epigraphe, "Vous, jeune homme, au bon sens avez vous dit adieu." Et cette Préface, "J'ai vingt ans, j'ai mal fait, je pourrai faire mieux."'

[3] Charles Vellay, 'Les poursuites contre l'*Organt*,' *Revue Bleue*, VIII, No. 8 (August 10, 1907), pp. 186–87.

the title *Esprit de la Révolution et de la Constitution de France*, it enjoyed immediate popularity, the edition selling out within a few days.[1]

The French people in the spring of 1791 were still firmly royalist. The flight of the king to Varennes, the foreign war, and the revelations of court treachery that were to shatter the throne, were still hidden in the future. Saint-Just's 'Spirit of the Revolution,' written at this time, was therefore a moderate work, not unfriendly to the monarchy, and in keeping with the constitutional royalism of his prospective constituents. It swept together the opinions of the day and expressed them convincingly, but with no great originality of thought. What signalized the brochure among a hundred others of similar nature was not the subject matter but the style. In its pages the dogmatic tenets of the revolutionary faith took on suddenly a new and thrilling certitude; glittering generalities hardened to the compactness of an aphorism; complex relationships grew luminous in a single phrase. It was the first sample of that swift laconic prose which had already marked Saint-Just out for fame, and was to make him, at twenty-five, one of the leading orators in the National Convention.

Eloquence is of all the arts the most ephemeral, but it is possible that Saint-Just's discourses suffer less in transcription than those of any other revolutionary orator. For he had only one style; he spoke exactly as he wrote, and his speeches were essays read from the tribune. A meticulous preparation, an infinite capacity for taking pains, condensed his prose to its amazing economy and energy. But such a method has its defects. Too often his finest passages smelled of the lamp; his metaphors were hard and cold, as if beaten out of frozen metal; his best epigrams had the air of carefully prepared impromptus. Given a respectful hearing, he never failed to convince, for

[1] Barère, *Mémoires*, IV, 407.

the march of his logic was inexorable. But to disarm a heckler with a witty retort, to cajole and flatter a hostile audience, were things beyond his skill. This was a weakness not merely of style but of character, and in the end, with the certainty of a Greek tragedy, it was destined to destroy him.

The autumn of 1791 brought with it the election for which all France was impatiently waiting. The National Assembly set a term to its labours, and the people were invited to elect a new legislature as provided in the recently completed constitution. Chosen to represent his district, Saint-Just hastened to Laon in September. He had a strong following and felt that his place among the deputies of the Department was assured. But his hopes were wrecked on a technicality. Twenty-five was the minimum age for a deputy, and he lacked it by eleven months. On this objection his name was stricken from the list of candidates, and even his privileges as an elector were annulled.[1]

The humiliation of this reverse flung Saint-Just into a mood of bitter despair. A conviction seized him that the Revolution would be over before he had a chance to play a part in it, and this fear was fed by the news from Paris. The members of the Constituent Assembly surrendered their seats with the relief of sailors who sight port after a weary voyage. 'The end of the Revolution has arrived,' Louis XVI affirmed, and even Robespierre echoed him 'The Revolution is ended.' Saint-Just read these declarations with a sinking heart, and saw his dream of fame deferred for an indefinite period, possibly forever. Those fortunate deputies who had preceded him to Paris would enjoy a two years' lease of power, while he was condemned for the same period to inglorious idleness. There was not even the hope that Louis might dissolve the Legislature

[1] *Bulletin historique et philologique du comité des travaux historiques et scientifiques* (Paris, 1902), pp. 152–53. Published by the Ministère de l'Instruction publique.

before its term was up and order a new election, for such a
step was forbidden by the Constitution of 1791.

The winter that followed seemed to Saint-Just the
longest that he had ever known. Even his zest for literature was gone. 'I am sick of myself,' he had written the
previous February, 'and this perpetual study, pursued in
solitude, is becoming an obsession.' [1] In this lengthening
exile the fanatical bent of his mind became more pro-
nounced, and his theories, unpruned by the shears of
reality, grew more ruthless and more radical. Had he gone
earlier to Paris, his revolutionary ardour might have
cooled, like that of many others who were radicals in
1789 and reactionaries in 1792. But he was condemned,
as it were, to dwell in a mirror world, and his thought took
on something of the squat perspective, the angular form
and deceptive lucidity of a looking-glass landscape. In
that rarefied atmosphere he felt himself slowly stifling.
The dust of battle was what he craved, not the dust of
books, and there was no comfort for him in living the
great adventure vicariously through the journals.

To pass the days he drilled the National Guard of the
canton, acquiring, by the spring of 1792, a dominating
influence in the company. On May 13 he harangued them
while they planted a tree of liberty, and on July 8 he took
command of the delegation chosen to celebrate the *Fête de
la Fédération*. This time, however, their destination was
not Paris, but Chauny, in their own Department, and the
Fête gave Saint-Just no opportunity, as in 1790, to watch
the Assembly in action. France, having drifted into war
with both Austria and Prussia, was threatened with invasion; on July 11 the Assembly proclaimed the Fatherland in danger. A military career was thus offered Saint-
Just, as an alternative to the legislative rôle so long denied
him. But he preferred to wait, his thoughts still fixed on

[1] Charles Vellay, 'Lettres inédites de Saint-Just,' *Revue historique de la
Révolution française*, I (1910), 481.

the arena in Paris. 'Nothing is so dear to the ear of Liberty,' he had written in 1791, 'as the tumult and shouting of an assembly of people. There the great spirits rouse themselves, there the unworthy are unmasked, there merit reveals itself in all its splendour and falsehood makes way before the truth.' [1]

Yet it is impossible to wait forever in the wings for a call that does not come. As Saint-Just saw the revolutionary drama swept daily into more passionate and starker scenes, his patience forsook him, and in bitter envy he began to curse those fortunate friends who had outstripped him in the race to Paris, yet would not help him to follow. A letter written at the close of July, 1792, to his compatriot Daubigny, in Paris, is a startling mirror of his mood.

I entreat you, my dear friend, to come to the Fête; I implore you; nevertheless, do not neglect your municipality. I have proclaimed here the destiny I divine for you: you will one day be a great man of the Republic. As for me, since I came here I have been fired with a republican fever that devours and consumes me.... It is a disaster that I cannot remain in Paris. I feel within me something which triumphs with the age. Companion of glory and of liberty, preach them in your sections; let danger be your inspiration. Go to see Desmoulins, embrace him for me, and tell him he will never see me again. That I esteem his patriotism, but that I scorn him because I have penetrated his soul and he fears that I shall betray him. Tell him not to abandon the good cause, enjoin it on him, for he lacks the courage of a magnanimous virtue. Farewell; I am above misfortune. I will endure anything, but I will tell the truth. You are all despicable, you who have not appreciated me. My palm, for all that, may some day rise and obscure yours! Infamous wretches that you are, I am a cheat, a rascal, because I have no money to give you. Tear out my heart and eat that. You will become what you are not at all: great!...

[1] O.C., I, 270.

O God, must Brutus languish forgotten, far from Rome! My resolution is made, however. If Brutus does not kill the others he will kill himself....

SAINT-JUST [1]

At the very moment his pen traced this furious letter (which it is possible he never sent, since it was found among his papers after Thermidor), Fate was throwing down the barriers on the road to his desire. The mismanagement of the war and the pressure of invasion had raised the French people to a sort of exalted madness; Louis was openly charged with betraying the nation to the enemy; and in July the publication of the Brunswick Manifesto dealt the final blow to his tottering throne. This bombastic proclamation from the headquarters of the Prussian Army warned the people of Paris that if they dared to harm the royal family their city would be given over to total annihilation. No further proof of collusion between the court and the invaders was necessary. On August 10 the mob stormed the Tuileries; Louis was driven to the Assembly, which suspended him; and the members of the Revolutionary Commune of Paris became the virtual dictators of France. Having sown the wind, the deputies of the Legislative Assembly were helpless before the whirlwind they were reaping. Since the chief of the executive power was a prisoner and the constitution useless, they summoned a National Convention to decide the form of government and the fate of the king. Thus, before half its session was over, the Legislative Assembly dissolved, and the voters of France were invited to participate in an extraordinary election.

This time Saint-Just had attained the required age. The electoral assembly for his Department opened its session at Soissons on September 2. While the Prussians were seizing Verdun, and the Paris mob, in its desperation,

[1] O.C., I, 348-49.

slaughtered sixteen hundred inmates of the prisons, Saint-Just at Soissons was pressing his campaign and rallying his forces. He was elected September 5, by a majority of 349 out of 600 votes, fifth deputy for the Department of the Aisne.[1] A week later he set out for Paris. No longer was Brutus to languish, forgotten, far from Rome. He had found his place in the assembly of the people, where merit would proclaim itself and falsehood make way before the truth.

[1] O.C., I, 350–51.

CHAPTER III

THE TRIAL OF TARQUIN

On ne peut point regner innocement.
Saint-Just, November 13, 1792.[1]

On September 21, 1792, the National Convention opened its first session. A bare half of the 750 deputies had arrived, but these hastened to declare royalty abolished in France. Four days later, as there appeared to be nothing else to do, they voted France a ꓹ ꓲublic, but with noticeably less enthusiasm. The indecision was typical. For a majority of the new deputies had come to Paris without any clear policy or party allegiance. Unorganized and unsure of themselves, they were to veer back and forth on the winds of discussion, until they yielded control of the Convention into the hands of a resolute minority.

In the long, bare hall of the *Salle de Manège*, which suggested an arena with its cleared centre and banks of mounting benches around the sides, the newcomers sought places for themselves. A majority drifted to the neutral middle section, facing the rostrum and the president's chair. There, in the 'Plain,' as it was called, they were to sit through the grim months of conflict, hugging their obscurity while the lightnings played above them. To their left, where the benches, sweeping around the end of the hall, climbed from six to nine rows, sat the Parisian deputies, the nucleus of the terrible 'Mountain.' On their right, less compact but more numerous, was the group which had controlled the previous assembly and was to dominate the first sessions of the new — the ill-fated Gironde.

Saint-Just took his place from the first among the men of the 'Mountain.' His acquaintanceship with Des-

[1] O.C., I, 369.

moulins, his admiration for Robespierre, and the natural impetuosity of his spirit drew him to the most radical group. Silent at first, he watched while orators of more fame and experience opened the discussions, and thus he learned to recognize by sight men whose names were already a legend. Danton, with his pock-marked face, burly figure, and volcanic eloquence, was to be seen almost daily at the rostrum. So, too, was the suave Barère, facile speaker on a variety of topics, whose soft words could smooth like oil the troubled waters of the Convention. Billaud-Varennes, exhaling his cold furies; Collot d'Herbois, the ex-actor, who had forsaken his comedian's rôle for more realistic tragedy and was stained like his friend Billaud with the infamy of the September massacres; the gentle Couthon, strangely out of place among these active figures, a cripple whom ambition was to convert into a regicide; and not least, the dapper Robespierre, powdered and pedantic, with his frigid manner and flashes of wasplike anger — all these men Saint-Just was to know better on the Committee of Public Safety. For the moment he stood aside and observed them, gauging their virtue, noting their words, their gestures, even their silences, and remembering everything with the fidelity of a recording angel.

His fellow Montagnards, in those opening weeks of the session, wore gloomy expressions. Developments in the Convention were little to their liking, for the Gironde, 'that Brissotin faction,' seemed destined to dominate the Assembly. For Brissot and his followers had been largely responsible for the outbreak of the war, which now took a surprising turn for the better. The Prussians, checked in the Ardennes, withdrew at the approach of winter, and the armies of the new republic pursued them to the Rhine and soon overran Belgium. The Girondists were swift to seize the credit for these late successes in a war they had been the first to advocate. They crowded all the important posts in the Assembly with their adherents, electing Pétion president, Condorcet vice-president, and Brissot and Vergniaud secretaries. Even the important Committee of the Constitution, which should have been as representative as possible, was two-thirds Girondist.[1]

At the Jacobin Club these reverses drew sour comments from the 'patriots.' This society, through its prestige and its affiliations, had made itself the most powerful political organization of the day. At its nightly sessions the deputies of Paris (Danton, Robespierre, Desmoulins, Collot d'Herbois and Billaud-Varennes) plotted to break the Girondist yoke. On October 10, Collot d'Herbois made a vicious attack on Brissot, who was forthwith expelled from the society. The Girondists retaliated in the Convention, where they denounced Marat, 'The People's Friend,' as a demagogue, accused Danton of inciting the September massacres, and hurled the insult *dictator* in Robespierre's face. The three Montagnard leaders swept aside these charges amid cheers from the Parisian sympathizers crowding the galleries. They had little love for each other, but the stupidity of the Girondist tactics drove them together. The Left, as an opposition party, was being unified by its grievances. It fell back on a policy of obstruction, while it waited for an issue on which it might challenge the Right with impunity.

The conflict of parties was in part a struggle between Paris and the provinces, for the Girondists desired to reduce the power of the capital and elevate that of the departments. Naturally this added nothing to their popularity with the Parisians, who frequently heckled and threatened them from the gallery when they spoke in the Convention, and jostled them in the streets. In self-defense, the Girondists proposed to call up a company of federal troops from all the departments, to preserve tranquillity, but the Jacobin deputies, having little to fear from

[1] F. A. Aulard, *Histoire politique de la Révolution française* (Paris, 1901), p. 268.

the mob, affected to find the suggestion sinister. It might forge a sword for the hand of tyranny, and place the populace at the mercy of a Prætorian Guard. Saint-Just, harkening to the debates on the project, decided that he had found a topic for his maiden speech in the Convention, and hastened to his rooms to write it; but before the discourse was polished to his liking, the discussion had moved on to other issues. Not to be frustrated, he carried the manuscript to the Jacobin Club, and read it at the meeting of October 22. The aim of his reasoning was to prove that an armed force would be a menace both to the deputies and the people. Moreover, the whole conception of military power, he argued, was foreign to the spirit of a deliberative body, which, 'like the gods, ought to rule by wisdom.'[1] As this sounded like an echo of the Jacobin motto *La force de la raison et la force du peuple, c'est la même chose,* the patriots raised the perfunctory cheer demanded by such an orthodox *cliché.* But the discourse as a whole had only a dubious success, bringing 'the citizen Sinjeu,' as the records tactfully phrased it, 'applause less vigorous than merited.'[2]

He learned rapidly. Two weeks later, when he addressed the Jacobins a second time, he had caught the trick of those lurid and ominous phrases which were the fuel of fanaticism. 'Citizens, I do not know what stroke is being prepared, but there is suspicion, there is tension everywhere. Paris is gorged with soldiers, and this at a time when the ex-king is about to face his trial.... All our woes are traceable to our political situation: when governments are moribund they teem with rascals like a corpse with worms.... I entreat the members of this and the sister societies to denounce all the traitors, so that the whole nation may quicken its vigilance and all the conspiracies be unmasked.'[3]

The ex-king was to be brought to trial! At last the

[1] O.C., I, 361.   [2] O.C., I, 353.   [3] O.C., I, 362–63.

Jacobins had found an issue upon which they could challenge the Girondist supremacy with some prospect of success. Their tactics were simple; they proposed to demand the death of Louis XVI with such brutal and insistent energy that, rather than yield to the dictation of a minority, the Right would have to resist, thus incurring the charge of royalism. The Girondists, who had led the attack on the king in the Legislative Assembly, were thus to be backed into their own fire; and the death of Louis, if they failed to save him, would leave them compromised beyond exculpation.

On November 3, the Convention debated the question whether Louis was responsible for his crimes and could be brought to trial. A host of objections beset the project: there was no court with powers adequate to try him, and no precedent for creating one. Nor, for that matter, could the king legally be impeached at all, since the Constitution of 1791 had guaranteed him immunity. The men of the Convention, lawyers most of them, were fascinated and troubled by these technicalities. Only a few had the courage to invoke the stern principle *salus populi suprema lex esto*, and demand the death of Louis as a measure of public safety, a necessary step in the consolidation of the Republic.

Of this resolute minority Saint-Just made one. On November 13, he startled the Convention with a maiden speech which left an ineffaceable impression upon his auditors. Few of the *conventionnels* knew, even by sight, the fair-haired, blue-eyed youth who moved austerely to the tribune in response to the president's nod. They noted casually the delicate contours of his face, his clear-cut profile, and the sombre gravity of his expression. A manuscript lay on the stand before him, but he scarcely glanced at it as he began to speak, calmly, in a level voice, without flourishes. The deliberate precision of his utterance masked the starkness of his demands, but underneath the polished phrases his thought marched to its conclusion, cold and sharp as the executioner's steel.

It was a judicial murder Saint-Just required of his colleagues, a decree of death, with no preliminaries and no reprieve. Louis's guilt, he stated simply, required no proof: *It is impossible to reign and be innocent.* To seek legal precedents where none existed was a waste of time: *There was nothing in the laws of Numa for judging Tarquin.* Quibbling over technicalities only delayed a vengeance too long overdue. *In such a trial* (ironic truth) *formalities are mere hypocrisy.* The death of Louis was necessary to assure the tranquillity of the nation; to sentence him at once was the one sane and politic course. 'People will one day stand amazed to learn that the eighteenth century was less advanced than the time of Cæsar; then the tyrant was slain in the open senate, with no more formality than three and twenty dagger strokes.' Louis had no rights, he was outside the law, an alien, an enemy, a Catiline, a murderer. 'Hasten, then, and pass judgment on the king,' was Saint-Just's final adjuration, 'for there is no citizen but has the right on him that Brutus had on Cæsar.'[1]

The *conventionnels* recoiled before such drastic logic, disliking, very probably, to have their duty prescribed for them by the youngest of their number in such mandatory terms. For a month thereafter the case of Louis was debated, postponed, and re-argued until the populace lost patience. On December 2, a delegation from the forty-eight sections of Paris crowded into the *Salle de Manège* with a demand for peremptory action. Bowing to the will of the sovereign people, the deputies hastened to vote that Louis was responsible for his crimes and should be brought to trial for them. The decree was a victory for the Left, a first-fruit of the understanding between the Jacobins and the mob. Stung by the reverse, the Girondists

[1] The complete discourse is printed in O.C., I, 365–72.

struck back obliquely, but their blows fell short. The initiative had definitely passed to their opponents.

The leaders of the Right still commanded a majority in the Convention when they took the trouble to concert their efforts, but their party lacked organization to such an extent that it can be called a party only by courtesy. As a result of this lack of unity, the Girondists lost ground with each new test of strength. On December 27, a Girondist, Salle, proposed that the fate of the king should be decided by a vote of the nation. 'We must be free,' he urged, 'to say to posterity that it was the whole of France and not the people of Paris that judged Louis XVI.' [1] This was a tactical move of the first order, for by a popular plebiscite the departments might save the king and rebuke the violence of the Paris mob. The Jacobins dared not concede the point, yet to refuse a plebiscite seemed like flouting the sovereignty of the people. As usual they masked their confusion by a display of fury, and accused the Right of trying to save Louis by plunging the nation into civil war. 'Let us dare to tell the truth,' Saint-Just commanded, 'the truth that burns in our hearts like a lamp in a tomb! This talk of faction is all designed to make you defer judgment because the monarchy is still alive among you.' [2] He insisted that each deputy should mount the tribune and reveal his heart by declaring Louis guilty or not guilty of the crimes charged against him.

At the proposal the galleries went wild with applause. It had appeared to the good citizens that their drama was in danger of being extinguished in provincial ballot boxes, while their royal victim escaped them. Saint-Just left the tribune amid a tumult of cheers and whistles so unseemly that the president of the Convention attempted a mild reproof. 'I would remind the citizens,' he ventured, when he could make his voice heard, 'that this is an affair of

[1] *Moniteur*, December 29, 1792.

[2] *Ibid.*, December 28, 1792.

tragic solemnity. Cheers and hisses are alike forbidden.'[1] But the citizens, who enjoyed their shows better with each day that passed, would not be silenced. They continued to cheer the Mountain and hiss the Gironde with unabashed enthusiasm, and Robespierre continued to assure them that the force of reason and the force of the people were the same thing. Against this combination of the Mountain and the mob the Girondists could make no progress. The party of the Left was still the weaker in numbers, but it had found the secret of popular support.

The formula, as in Roman times, was *panem et circenses*. The sessions of the Convention, the civic *fêtes*, and the guillotine provided entertainment for the mob, and as early as November Saint-Just had demanded cheaper bread. The inflation of the currency, he pleaded, was working untold hardship on the poor, and the only means of lessening it would be to print no more *assignats*, and to decree the free circulation of grain throughout the Republic. His speech appeared to weary a majority of the deputies, but it won the approval of the intelligent and captious Marat, 'The People's Friend.' 'The only orator who has afforded me any pleasure in the tribune,' the latter wrote, 'is Saint-Just. His *Discours sur les subsistances* reveals style, logic and vision. When he has been ripened by reflection, and has rid himself of affectations, he will be a man. He is a thinker.'[2] Saint-Just, indeed, had arraigned his colleagues in magisterial fashion on their neglect of duty. 'It is time,' he urged, 'that we laboured for the happiness of the people. Legislators who are to bring light and order into the world must pursue their course with inexorable tread, fearless and unswerving as the sun.'[3] Robespierre, with whom Saint-Just was always in close agreement, supported the decree for the free circulation

---

[1] *Archives parlementaires*, LV, 710.
[2] Jean Jaurès, ed., *Histoire socialiste*, IV, 860, quotes the passage.
[3] O.C., I, 383.

of grain with long-winded eloquence. The solicitude of the Montagnards for the sufferings of the people wearied the Right; their arguments were addressed to the galleries and their opponents knew it. 'When the people demand bread,' jeered Barbaroux, 'we can give them Robespierre's speeches.' [1] Yet the tactics told. The Girondists found themselves stigmatized as bourgeois, friends of privilege, gentlemen who wished to preserve in the Republic a moneyed aristocracy.

Their growing unpopularity was reflected more and more clearly in the jeers and hisses of the galleries; some of them were threatened with violence when they appeared on the street. Fear and pressure told on their ranks when the fate of Louis came to the final vote, and told even more upon the vacillating deputies of the Plain. On January 15, the question of the King's guilt was posed. No one dared attempt to exculpate him; the verdict was a unanimous affirmative. The motion to appeal his sentence to the people for ratification was then laid before the Convention, but it failed to carry. A majority of the deputies, having declared Louis guilty, were prepared to accept the responsibility for his punishment.

At eight o'clock on the evening of January 17, the final vote commenced. Since morning the galleries had been crowded with spectators eager to witness the closing act of the judicial drama, and the *gendarmes* of the Convention were apparently unable to prevent the bolder members of this audience from wandering about the hall and even joining the *conventionnels* on their benches. Each deputy as he climbed the steps of the rostrum to deliver his verdict was greeted with a tumult of exhortations, and stepped down, if he failed to vote for death, under a rain of epithets. Yet the presence in the audience of a rowdy element, drunk on brandy and excitement, does not quite explain or quite excuse the final verdict: for that the

[1] *Archives parlementaires*, LIV, 47–48.

Girondists could blame their own inconsistency. The *appel nominal* commenced with the Department of Haute-Garonne; that of the Gironde came third. The deputies from Bordeaux thus had an opportunity to set an example of clemency at the commencement of the balloting which might have crystallized the decision of many a wavering spirit in the Plain. Yet of the eight members of the Girondist Party hailing from that department, five of them — Boyer-Fonfrède, Ducos, Gensonné, Guadet and Vergniaud — voted for death. They hoped, it may be, to regain by this final ruthlessness some of their lost ascendency in the Convention, but if so their political instinct was at fault. It was the death warrant of their party which they had voted, and their own. In sending Louis XVI to the guillotine all five set their feet upon the same path.

The pangs of indecision which tortured so many conscientious deputies during the fateful hours that preceded the final vote left Saint-Just apparently untroubled. There is no evidence that he felt a moment's irresolution concerning his qualifications as a magistrate or the penalty to be inflicted. 'If I did not hold from the people the right to judge the tyrant, I would hold it from Nature,' he affirmed simply, in casting his vote against a ratification by popular plebiscite.[1] When the moment came to pronounce the capital sentence he spoke with the same grave air of conviction. 'Because Louis XVI was the enemy of the people, of their liberty and their happiness, my conclusion is for death.'[2]

To Vergniaud, as president of the Convention for that fortnight, fell the task of announcing the results of the *appel nominal*. Of the 721 deputies voting, a narrow majority favoured the death penalty. Many people still hoped for a reprieve; the question was posed January 20, but the Montagnards were resolute in their hour of victory. Louis was guillotined the following morning.

[1] *Archives parlementaires*, LVII, 90.   [2] *Ibid.*, LVII, 384.

CHAPTER IV

ACROSS THE RUBICON

*Le fragile édifice du gouvernement provisoire tremble sous vos pas;
l'ordre présent est le désordre mis en lois.*

SAINT-JUST, January 28, 1793.[1]

THE news of the king's execution shocked people in the provincial sections of France almost as much as it did the foreign courts. In the Convention the passions excited by the trial were suddenly stilled in the presence of the final tragedy while the deputies peered fearfully into the future. They had hurled the Revolution abruptly down an unknown road; henceforth, for these regicides, there would be no retreat from the way they had chosen. The Powers, already alarmed at the French annexation of Avignon and Nice, and the invasion of Belgium and Holland, pledged themselves to destroy this Republic which had made itself an Ishmael among the nations. It is little wonder if the deputies forgot for a few days their fratricidal contests and watched with apprehensive gaze for some darkening of the heavens as a portent of the fate they might expect.

The leaders of the Left were the first to recover a measure of audacity; they fronted the consequences of their victory with an air of stern defiance. 'One does not make revolutions by halves,'[2] declared Saint-Just: the words were to prove a knell for the hopes of all those, from Dumouriez to Danton, who sought to arrest the Revolution before its course was run. To the Montagnards the death of the king meant more than a parliamentary victory, for it condemned France to a long siege of terror and committed the destinies of the nation into their

[1] O.C., I, 405.   [2] O.C., I, 414.

hands. Some weeks earlier, Saint-Just had spoken of the necessity 'of opening the eyes of the French people to the virtues, too long ignored, of the minority who sat on the Mountain.'[1] What words had failed to achieve, deeds were now to accomplish, for the Rubicon once crossed, the Revolution was swept towards a crisis in which only men of pitiless decision could save it. The Girondists, divided, uncertain, hesitant before the conclusions of their own logic, were to be driven to the wall by their more ruthless and more realistic opponents.

The foreign war, which had come almost to a standstill, blazed up again at the news of the king's death, with a gravity that obscured all other issues. Prussia and Austria, already in the field for a year, were joined by Great Britain, Spain and Portugal. To meet this coalition of kings the Republic could oppose only a disorganized army which desertions had reduced by half. On January 1 the Convention appointed a Committee of General Defense to study a way out of the difficulties; and at the end of the month, with invasion threatening at every point of the frontier and coastline, the deputies recollected their committee and demanded a report. Sieyès, as spokesman, outlined a project whereby the Minister of War was to be invested with full authority for the equipment and direction of the armies, and was to be responsible to the Provisory Executive Council. Under the existing circumstances, it was imperative to centralize the control of military affairs, but Sieyès' suggestion for achieving this end found little favour on the benches of the Left. The reason for the Jacobin hostility Saint-Just hastened to make plain.

'The control of the military power,' he warned his colleagues, '(I do not say the direction of the manœuvres) is the inalienable right of the legislature.... I insist that the authority entrusted by Sieyès to the Council, that is to

[1] O.C., I, 400.

all the Ministers collectively, concerning the general operations of the war, shall be taken into your own hands.... I propose, in conclusion, that the Minister of War report directly to the National Convention, and be distinct from the Council.' [1]

The Council, or Provisory Executive Council, to give its full title, had been appointed the previous August to carry on the executive functions of the government after the suspension of the king. The Ministers who composed it were nominees of the Gironde, which fact in itself would explain Saint-Just's anxiety to curtail its powers. But party prejudices aside, Saint-Just's political instinct was sound, and he was correct in thinking that the Council of Ministers had neither the prestige nor the energy to direct the war. A majority of the members in the Convention apparently shared his conviction, for after considerable discussion it was decided that a radical reorganization of the Ministry of War was inadvisable on the eve of renewed hostilities. The melancholy consequence was that Sieyès' whole report was laid aside and no constructive alternative offered. Confusion continued to spread in the armies, despite the efforts of Beurnonville, the Minister of War, who laboured in vain to clear his department of parasites and infuse some energy into the administration.

In the middle of February, Saint-Just again addressed the Convention on the subject of the army. Dubois-Crancé, speaking on behalf of the Committee of War, had proposed the reorganization of the infantry battalions and the amalgamation of regular and volunteer units. Distinctions between new and old recruits were to be eliminated, and the officers of the lower grades elected by the rank and file. Saint-Just supported these recommendations as warmly as if he could already foresee, springing from them, the stalwart armies of the Republic with which Carnot was to organize the victories of the Year II. 'I

[1] O.C., I, 406.

know of but one method of resisting Europe,' he concluded, 'and that is to oppose to it the genius of liberty. Some have urged that the military elections will weaken and divide the army, but I am convinced, on the contrary, that in this way its strength ought to be multiplied.' [1] Mad as the experiment seemed, and subversive of all discipline, its application proved him right. The soldiers not only respected and obeyed the officers of their own choosing, but picked them as a rule with wisdom.

On February 24, the Convention issued a call for 300,-000 men, to be chosen by lot, and on March 8 it voted to send two of its members to each of the eighty-five departments to supervise the enrollment of the new levy. Saint-Just's discourses on military affairs had apparently won him some attention, for his name was second on the list of deputies chosen. He set out at once for the Departments of the Aisne and the Ardennes, in company with Jean Louis Deville, whom he remembered, no doubt, from his months at the School of Law in Rheims. Of their mission together no record appears to have survived beyond two letters which Deville wrote the Convention. In the second of these he described the wholly inadequate provision which had been made for the new draft of men, and laid the blame on the Minister of War. [2] Deville also mentioned the absence of his colleague. Saint-Just was on his way back to Paris, to present in person, with his customary energy, the evidences of negligence and confusion which his mission had revealed.

He appeared before the Committee of General Defense on April 1, and read a report (unfortunately lost) on the unpreparedness of the frontier departments to resist an invasion.[3] The disorganization which he had witnessed

[1] O.C., I, 413.

[2] *Recueil des actes du Comité de salut public*, II, 305. Edited by F. A. Aulard, 26 volumes, Paris, 1889–1923.

[3] *Ibid.*, III, 2.

among the troops on the Belgian border had shocked Saint-Just's orderly mind and roused dark apprehensions which he hastened to confide to the Jacobin Club. 'I announce to the Society,' he affirmed bluntly, 'that Beurnonville is a traitor. Citizens, I have not found a single man of virtue in the government; I have found good only among the people. It is time, not to unmask Beurnonville, but to smash the mask into his face without raising it.'[1] The patriots at the Club were loud in their applause, for Beurnonville, in his efforts to reform the Ministry of War, had deprived some of them of their sinecures in that Department, and he was involved also in the odium of the March defeats.

The suspicion long nursed by the Jacobins that all was not well at French army headquarters had received in those mad March days a staggering confirmation. At the end of January the Convention had ordered the General-in-chief, Dumouriez, to march on Holland, but the offensive had rapidly degenerated into a retreat. By the opening of March the Austrians had reconquered the greater part of Belgium. Liège surrendered to them on the 10th, and on the 18th Dumouriez risked and lost a battle at Neerwinden. In his disgust at the regicide Convention which he held responsible for his reverses, the general then deserted to the enemy, taking several of his staff officers with him. This act of treachery was a fatal blow to the Girondist Party which had nominated Dumouriez to command and kept him in power. 'There has never been a single circumstance in which Brissot failed to defend Dumouriez,' Robespierre declared with venomous satisfaction on April 3. 'The system of Dumouriez has been to involve us in a disastrous conflict in order to make it turn against liberty.... I insist that the first measure of safety which we must take is a decree against all those who are accused of complicity with Dumouriez, and es-

[1] O.C., I, 417.

pecially against Brissot.'[1] But the Convention was not yet prepared to decimate itself and Robespierre's motion was rejected. He was to see it pass before two months were out.

To the military reverses in Belgium and Alsace was added the burden of a counter-revolution in the West and South of France. The peasants of the Vendée, who had been excited by the decrees against the priests, and shocked by the execution of the king, were goaded into open rebellion by the attempts at military conscription. They flung themselves into a royalist revolt which threatened in a few weeks to sweep from the Loire to the Rhone. During those dark days in the spring of 1793 it seemed almost certain that Paris was fated to be crushed between two converging battle lines, and the leaders of the Revolution given over to the sanguinary reprisals which the royalists had promised them.

The news of these disasters shocked the Convention into measures at once vindictive and salutary. The famous Revolutionary Tribunal was erected to judge royalists, enemy agents and counter-revolutionaries; the rebels of the West were proclaimed *hors de loi*; and a Revolutionary Army of the Interior was created to put down the revolting Departments. It was imperative, however, that the Convention should do more than organize the army and the Tribunal; it had also to organize itself. 'The Revolution will perish,' Saint-Just had pointed out in January, 'if the departments of the provisory administration lack a concerted impulse and a centre of activity, for principles and ideas of liberty are no substitute for harmony in a government.... Today the executive power which governs the Republic is either too inept to organize, direct or repress anything, or else it lacks the authority.'[2] Two months of dispute and disaster were needed to drive home the

[1] *Archives parlementaires*, LXI, 273.
[2] O.C., I, 402.

truth of these observations before the deputies could bring themselves to act upon them.

In the Constitution of 1791, in accordance with the opinions of Montesquieu, the Executive, Legislative and Judicial branches of the government had been clearly defined and separated. But in the National Convention, which was an extraordinary body called to control the country in a crisis, and to prepare a new constitution, these careful distinctions were difficult to maintain. The deputies had usurped judicial functions in judging the king; and their further acts constantly encroached upon the limits of the executive power which was vested in the Provisory Executive Council. The Council could not resist this steady encroachment, for the ministers who composed it, chosen outside the Convention and generally unpopular, were in fact little more than impotent scapegoats who bore the blame for the misfortunes which they were help-less to avert. It was essential, as Saint-Just had urged, to provide the administration with a concerted impulse and a centre of activity if the Revolution was to be saved. Only the Convention had the prestige and the authority to attempt such a concentration of power, but the Convention, despite the invocations of Danton, Marat, Robes-pierre — and Saint-Just — continued to hesitate and de-lay in a spirit of suicidal irresolution.

An assembly of seven hundred men, debating in public and rent by factions, was obviously too unwieldy a machine to govern a nation at war. Yet the deputies stubbornly refused to recognize the fact, or to delegate an adequate share of their jealously guarded authority to an executive committee. When the growing danger made some degree of centralization imperative, they had contented them-selves with a half-measure, and organized at the beginning of January the inept Committee of General Defense. This council of twenty-four members only reproduced on a smaller scale the factional controversies of the Convention, and was paralyzed by a mania for discussion. Girondist in complexion at first, it was renewed on March 25 with the two parties evenly represented, and its nullity thereby assured beyond all question. The members, realizing that they might be called to account for the misfortunes in Belgium and the Vendée, over which they had no control, begged to be replaced. 'At this moment,' declared their spokesman, Isnard, on April 5, 'the executive power has no existence.... The committee which you have appointed is incapable of any good.... It has itself demanded that you organize another committee in such a way that it can perform the functions for which it is created. I demand an immediate discussion on the matter, and I hereby resign from the Committee of General Defense.' [1]

The solution, quite clearly, lay in a smaller committee endowed with more adequate powers. The deputies disliked the thought of creating a despotic committee, and laying their necks beneath the knife of its displeasure, but they disliked even more the fate that awaited them in the event of a successful counter-revolution. Barère the mediator helped them to choose what seemed to be the lesser of the two evils. He proposed the election of a Committee of Public Safety, appointed to exercise a simple power of surveillance, to deliberate on urgent matters, propose measures to the Convention, and stimulate the moribund Executive Council to action. To allay any fears of a dictatorship, Barère pointed out that such a committee would have no authority over civil liberties, no control of the finances, no powers at all independent of the National Convention. It could, moreover, be renewed each month by a special vote, and changed or discontinued the moment that it threatened to grow arrogant. Burdened with these limitations the Committee of Public Safety was established on April 6. It included nine members of

[1] *Moniteur*, April 8, 1793.

the Convention: Danton, Barère, Delmas, Bréard, Cambon, Jean-de-Bry, Guyton-Morveau, Treilhard and Robert Lindet.

The dominating personality in this first Committee of Public Safety was Danton, and the Committee, during the three months that it remained in power, was in reality a Danton cabinet. The ends for which he worked were the reconciliation of the parties within the Convention and the reëstablishment of peace with Europe. Danton hoped to arrest and stabilize the Revolution, and to extricate France from the war by a combination of force and diplomacy. He failed in both aims, for the Girondists repulsed his overtures and the Mountain grew suspicious of his negotiations with the European courts. Peace talk appeared like treachery when the Austrians were battering down the French fortresses on the frontier, and Danton's temporizing measures were further blamed for the spread of the rebellion in the Vendée. It was his misfortune to take office when the tide of disaster had not quite reached the full, but the responsibility for his failure and his fall from power was also in a peculiar sense his own. Harbouring few rancours himself, he could not gauge the factional hatreds of the Assembly and he tried to support his cabinet on a coalition platform. He misjudged the depth and fury of the revolutionary stream, believing in May, 1793, that the time had come for compromise and consolidation. That was his error. One does not make revolutions by halves.

CHAPTER V

THE LAWS OF MINOS

Le jour où je me serai convaincu qu'il est impossible de donner au peuple français des mœurs douces, énergiques, sensible, et inexorables pour la tyrannie et l'injustice, je me poignarderai.

SAINT-JUST.[1]

THE excitement which surrounded the trial of the king so far obscured all other issues that it was February before the National Convention turned to consider seriously the task for which it had been specially convoked — the drafting of a new constitution. This delay was not unpleasing to the deputies, for they were too jealous of their little brief authority to hasten a work the completion of which would mean a new election. The Committee of the Constitution, appointed early in October, 1792, took four months to prepare a preliminary draft, and this, when laid before the Convention in February, was immediately criticized. No good, the Jacobins were convinced, could come out of a committee dominated by Girondists, and Condorcet's project, so lengthy that it exhausted him to read it, was rejected as unsatisfactory by deputies who had yawned through the ordeal of listening to it.

The constitutional question was thereupon thrown open to debate once more, and the deputies invited to present their own projects. This meant, in the tense and heated atmosphere of the sessions, that the issue would be buried under floods of acrimony and abuse. No irreconcilable disagreement separated the Gironde and the Mountain on the basic problems of the constitution, but the will to differ drove them to magnify every minor clash of opinion. Thus the Girondists strove to rally to their support the richer elements of the bourgeoisie by accusing

[1] O.C., II, 504.

the Jacobins of a plan to conscript wealth — a pernicious charge, dangerous enough to draw from Robespierre an exasperated denial. 'Souls of mud,' he upbraided them, 'I don't want to touch your treasures, however unclean their origin.' [1] The Girondists, in their turn, were thrown on the defensive by the charge that they sought to depose Paris from its position of leadership and reduce its influence in the Republic to that of a single department, one among eighty-five. To the French people at large these endless arguments brought the suspicion that the deputies were deliberately wasting their time, and by April the Convention found itself urged from all sides to terminate the period of confusion by the adoption of a definitive constitution.

It is possible, in reviewing these early years of the Revolution, to speak without exaggeration of a 'Constitutional Cult,' so firm was the faith reposed in wise legislation, and so extravagant the blessings expected from it. Saint-Just, who was a convert and apostle of this particular form of idolatry from his school days, reflects in his writings the fascination which it possessed for the doctrinaire mind. The legislator he envisaged as a godlike being who commanded the future. 'You who make the laws,' he reminded his colleagues more than once, 'the vices and the virtues of the people will be your work.' [2] Steeped in the writings of Montesquieu, Rousseau and the Physiocrats, he revered the wise lawgiver as a physician who could cure all the ills of the body politic, and assure, by prescribing a rational regimen, the perpetual health and prosperity of a nation. Nature, he believed, had established rational laws to govern men in society no less than stars in space; the legislator was a sort of Newton of the social order who had merely to discover the basic principles of his science and the millennium would be achieved. It was

[1] *Archives parlementaires*, LXIII, 197. April 24, 1793.
[2] O.C., I, 380; 419-20.

necessary, not to *make* laws, but to *discover* them, to codify the eternal verities implicit in the nature of things. 'Every political edict which is not based upon nature,' Saint-Just proclaimed with his usual succinctness, 'is wrong.' [1]

The light of reason, playing upon the chaos of the old régime, was to shape from it, in the dawn of a new creation, the ideal republic of the future. His mind suffused with the ardour of this Platonic dream, Saint-Just grew lyrical, comparing the might of the legislator to 'that changeless radiance which determines the form of all things.' The social turmoil of the Revolution was to be stilled by the magic of pure reason. 'When a people, having become free, establish wise laws, their revolution is complete....' [2]

In harbouring these illusions, Saint-Just was in no way original. His receptive mind had merely absorbed a little too literally the dogmas of the day. A constitution was commonly regarded as the crowning achievement of the Revolution because it was expected to embody for all time the verities so newly vindicated, and thus to become a charter of liberties for all mankind. In the spirit of contagious optimism then prevalent, it was taken for granted that all right-thinking men would find themselves in agreement on the fundamental issues, and that the new institutions would command universal acceptance, since they would be based upon principles as self-evident as the axioms of Euclid. The legislator who first sketched the charter of the new state would be ranked by a grateful posterity with Minos and Lycurgus and Numa. From his godlike mind the new republic was expected to spring full-armed and perfect as Pallas herself, created by the pure force of harmonious thought. 'Peace and prosperity,' wrote Saint-Just, 'public virtue, victory, everything is in the vigour of the laws. Outside of the laws everything is sterile and dead.' [3]

To shatter to bits the sorry scheme of things as he

[1] O.C., I, 306.   [2] O.C., I, 264.   [3] O.C., I, 419.

found it, and remould it in the interest of the poor and the wretched, was a dream worth fighting for, and Saint-Just possessed his full share of the abstract humanitarianism of the eighteenth century. Like Robespierre, he questioned the right of society to inflict the death penalty; the use of torture in the courts he condemned vehemently; and the fate of bastards, compelled to bear a stigma of unmerited shame, moved him to tears. The responsibility of the state for the welfare of the poor he accepted and advocated with a vigour that ranks him among the early socialists. 'If you wish a republic,' he urged, 'so order it that the people may have the heart to be virtuous; for there are no political virtues without self-respect, and it is impossible to be self-respecting in the midst of poverty.' [1] Shortly before his death he confessed, 'I have the fond hope that the name of a friend of humanity ought one day to be held dear.' [2] It was an amiable weakness in one who boasted that he had left all weakness behind. Perhaps it was this compassion for humanity that made him so pitiless to men.

The spectacle of a legislative assembly in session, with all its pettiness and confusion, should have taught him humour and cynicism; instead it made him more dogmatic. Towards the end of April, he decided to enter the discussions on the constitution himself, and he prepared a careful recapitulation of his views on the subject. This *Discours sur la constitution à donner à la France* he prefaced with a confession of his faith; the revolutionary creed has seldom found a more eloquent advocate.

It has always seemed to me [he wrote] that the social order was implicit in the very nature of things, and required nothing more from the human spirit than care in arranging the various elements; that a people could be governed without being made thralls or libertines or victims thereby; that man was born for

[1] O.C., I, 374.   [2] O.C., II, 494.

peace and liberty, and became miserable and cruel only through
the action of insidious and oppressive laws. And I believe therefore that if man be given laws which harmonize with the dictates
of nature and of his heart he will cease to be unhappy and
corrupt....

The legislator commands the future; to be feeble will avail
him nothing; it is for him to will what is good and to perpetuate
it; to make man what he desires him to be: for the laws, working
upon the social body, which is inert in itself, can produce either
virtue or crime, civilized customs or savagery. The virtues of
the Lacedemonians were in the heart of Lycurgus, the instability
of the Cretans in the heart of Minos.[1]

Concluding this *apologia*, Saint-Just presented to the
Convention the draft of a constitution which he had composed himself. 'A feeble essay,' he offered modestly,
'which may suggest ideas to those who think better than
I.' In reality, the project was a carefully worked-out plan
which might, under happier circumstances, have proved
of practical value. The form of government he advocated
was bicameral, consisting of a Legislative Assembly of
341 delegates chosen by universal manhood suffrage, and
a Council of 85 chosen by the electoral assemblies of the
Departments. The Council was to enforce the laws through
its nine ministers and various agents; but in his anxiety
to keep a check on the executive power Saint-Just made this
branch of the government too feeble and too complicated
to prove serviceable, and rendered impossible the degree
of centralization necessary in the conduct, for instance,
of a war.[2]

Unknown to himself, Saint-Just was climbing, through
his activity in the constitutional debates, the final steps
to power. For the long rift in the Convention was about
to be healed by force, leaving the Jacobins triumphant,

[1] O.C., I, 419–20.

[2] The *Essai de constitution* and the speech of presentation are printed in O.C.,
I, 418–54.

and out of this struggle the leaders of the Mountain emerged as dictators. The six turbulent weeks between May 24 and July 10 carried Saint-Just into the Committee of Public Safety, and set his feet on that heroic and strenuous road which was to end one year later at the foot of the guillotine. Some time within that period the young theorist and doctrinaire was metamorphosed into the man of action. The way had been prepared for this change, no doubt, yet its swiftness, though paralleled in the cases of some of the other terrorists, is none the less perturbing. In May Saint-Just was pondering the abstract bases of government; in July he was calmly invoking a decree of death against nine of his fellow deputies.

In the tragic developments of May 31–June 2, Saint-Just appears to have had no part. The insurrection of the Paris mob, the popular demand for the arrest of the 'Twenty-two' Girondists, and the final ignominious capitulation of the Convention when it voted the decree of June 2 under the threat of Hanriot's cannon, might well have shaken his serene faith in the power of the Legislator and the goodness of the People. But it is possible that he was not present at these melancholy sessions, for he had been summoned to collaborate on a task of high importance, a task which may well have absorbed his full attention and shut him away from the tumult and the shouting in the silence of a committee room.

On May 29, Barère proposed to the Convention that five additional members should be elected to the Committee of Public Safety for the purpose of drafting the constitution which had already been so long and so impatiently awaited. The following day Cambon announced that the Committee had selected five men for this duty, and named Hérault-Séchelles, Ramel-Nogaret, Couthon, Saint-Just and Mathieu. The appointments were promptly confirmed by the Convention, and the new sub-committee was instructed to prepare, in the shortest possible time, the project of a constitution. It was to be reduced to single articles, and ordered in such form as would best assure the unity, indivisibility and liberty of the Republic, and the rights of the people.

These five young Solons — their ages ran from twenty-five to thirty-six — were to complete in eight days a task over which the Convention had exercised itself for eight months. Saint-Just's inclusion in the committee was a signal tribute to his talents, for his colleagues were all his seniors in age and in experience. Hérault-Séchelles had been *avocat général* of the *Parlement de Paris* at the outbreak of the Revolution; Couthon and Mathieu had also won distinction in the legal profession; while Ramel-Nogaret, after serving in the Constituent Assembly, had presided for a year over the district tribunal at Carcassonne. In such a company Saint-Just had to accept a minor rôle, and the draft of the constitution prepared by the joint efforts of the five shows little direct evidence of his participation. One clause, Article XVIII, which states that the law cannot recognize domestic servitude, but only a free contract between the man who labours and the man who employs him, parallels so closely in word and thought the third article of Chapter III in his own draft of April, 1793, it may with some assurance be ascribed to him. Other contributions he must have made in the course of the deliberations; but he never boasted of his share in the labours of the committee, nor did he offer to defend the finished work before the Convention. Perhaps it offended his vanity to accept a minor place, and to see Hérault win all the acclaim. Nine months later, when he denounced Hérault before the Convention, Saint-Just tried to strip him of all credit in this matter. 'Hérault,' he affirmed, 'was a silent and unsympathetic witness to the work of those who traced the plan of the constitution.' This was a deliberate falsehood. The original draft of the constitution is entirely in Hérault's hand.[1]

[1] O.C., II, 327. E. Dard, *Hérault de Séchelles* (Paris, 1907), p. 227.

The Constitution of 1793 was an emergency measure, to be prepared, as the decree of May 30 ordered, 'in the shortest possible time.' But the five *rédacteurs* felt that the masterpiece of legislation upon which they were engaged ought to be distinguished by a classic concision and brevity of style, and they determined to model it upon some of the famous constitutions of antiquity. Saint-Just's reverence for the antique would not permit him to forget Minos, Numa and Lycurgus at such a moment, and it may well have been at his suggestion that Hérault despatched the following note to the Keeper of the Printed Books and Manuscripts at the Bibliothèque Nationale. The amazing missive bears the date of June 7.

Citizen:
    Charged with four of my colleagues to present by Monday the plan of a constitution, I pray you, in their names and mine, to procure for us immediately the *Laws of Minos* which should be obtainable in a collection of Greek laws. We have urgent need of them.[1]

In default of this mythical codex, Hérault and his coadjutors had to content themselves with imitating the laconic style of Lycurgus, and completed by June 9 a short constitution of ninety-seven articles which was presented to the Convention the following day. The deputies of the Mountain hastened to unite their voices in praise of the project, which was so full of noble sentiments, and was expressed, as Barère felicitously observed, 'in a style truly lapidary, the style of the Twelve Tables.'[2] During the sessions that followed, clause after clause was submitted to the Assembly, debated, amended, and passed; and when opposition threatened to develop on the Right among the stricken remnant of the Gironde, it was silenced

---

[1] Edmond Biré, *Journal d'un Bourgeois de Paris pendant la terreur* (5 volumes, Paris, 1895–1911), III, 50.

[2] *Archives parlementaires*, LXVI, 264. June 10, 1793. The first draft of the Constitution is printed on pages 256–64.

by a promise of imprisonment for any who dared to interrupt the proceeding once the discussion had been closed. The men who trod on the Mountain had possessed themselves of the law and the way of the transgressor was hard. On June 24 the final version of the Constitution, expanded to one hundred twenty-four articles, was forced through the Convention, and the news announced to the expectant populace by a salvo of cannon.

The explanation of this insistent haste was to be found in the rapid spread of revolt in the Departments, where the news of the decree of June 2 against the Girondists had excited grave opposition. The leaders of the Mountain were of the opinion that the proclamation of a democratic constitution would prove the speediest method of quieting the apprehensions stirred up by the violence of the Paris Commune. The document was stuffed with liberal promises, including universal suffrage and annual elections. It was proposed to ratify it by a national plebiscite, and, if the Constitution were accepted, to hold a special fête to mark its adoption. August 10, the first anniversary of the fall of the throne, was fixed as the date for the celebration.

It was an occasion worthy to be enlivened by all the pompous pageantry dear to the revolutionary orators. On the Place de la Bastille, the painter David designed, in the austere Egyptian style, a massive statue of Nature, from the breasts of which two streams of water, crystal clear, splashed into a wide basin beneath. Hérault-Séchelles, as President of the Convention that fortnight, represented the legislators whose ardent toil had wrested her secrets from this ancient Sphinx, and he led the way in pledging the Constitution from an onyx cup, which he filled at Nature's sparkling though uninspiring streams. He was followed by delegates from the eighty-seven Departments of the Republic, called to Paris specially to join in this Fête of Regeneration, and as each drank the fraternal toast he was greeted with the thunder of artillery.

A final discharge of cannon announced the departure of a procession, bearing with it in a cedar ark the Constitutional Act. Behind the ark flocked the deputies of the National Convention, each laden with a bouquet of grain and fruits. They were surrounded on all sides by the delegates of the Departments, who were tied together with streamers of tri-coloured ribbon to symbolize the unity of the French Republic. Upon reaching the Tuileries, the ark with its contents was borne reverently into the hall of the Convention, and laid in a square shrine prepared for it near the president's seat. There it was destined to remain. It had served its purpose in the pacification of the Departments, and its sublime and draconic principles were never to be compromised by the test of practical application.

CHAPTER VI

THE DECEMVIRATE

C'est le feu de la liberté qui nous a épurés, comme le bouillonnement des métaux chasse du creuset l'écume impure.

SAINT-JUST, July 8, 1793.[1]

THE fall of the Gironde was followed five weeks later by a reorganization of the Danton Cabinet. The triumphant Mountain required that period of time to consolidate its victory before it seized control of the central instrument of government, for Robespierre was no friend of recklessness and liked to have all his pieces in position before he made a move. He knew how vulnerable the most virtuous citizen became the moment he accepted an office of responsibility; and knowing this, he had a double motive for caution, foreseeing that events, if allowed to take their course, would speedily discredit the policy of the Dantonists, and by driving them from the Committee of Public Safety, prepare the way for his own advent.

This inclination to hasten slowly accounts for the delay shown in the prosecution of the fallen Girondists. Of the twenty-nine deputies confined to their lodgings by the decree of June 2, twelve fled before they could be arrested, and eight more evaded their guards during the month of June and slipped away from Paris. The hope of the fugitives was to rally their Departments against the Jacobin dictatorship. Some threw in their lot with the rebels of the Vendée; and even those who held aloof from a movement tinged with royalism earned the charge of being counter-revolutionaries, federalists and liberticides. Their flight from justice, which compromised their cause and destroyed the sympathy felt for them in many quarters, strengthened

[1] O.C., II, 28.

proportionately the position of their opponents. Yet the Jacobins wisely forbore to strike any ruthless blows at their victims during June. They desired first to pacify some of the agitation in the Departments by the proclamation of the new Constitution. The plebiscite indicated that a large majority of the electorate favoured the Constitutional Act, and the Jacobins exploited this as a proof that the nation welcomed their leadership. In reality, the nation had voted, or believed it had voted, the end of the 'revolutionary' régime and the adoption of a regular government under the 'Constitution of the Year I.' 'The people see in it the end of all their misfortunes,' the rational Carnot admitted June 30. 'It is worth the winning of twenty battles.'[1] The Convention, using the excuse of the war, chose to disregard the significance of the plebiscite and maintain the revolutionary government.

The Committee of Public Safety, Dantonist in composition and conciliatory in spirit, had no desire to punish the Girondists. Although the Convention, in arresting the Twenty-nine, had requested a report within three days, the Committee temporized for nearly three weeks. On June 15 it chose Cambon, Delmas and Saint-Just as a subcommittee to supervise the repressive measures planned against the rebels of the West; and on the 19th Saint-Just was instructed to prepare a report on the imprisoned deputies. But when he presented his draft on June 24, the Committee found it unsatisfactory; he had to work over it for a week before it was approved at the session of July 2; and another week was allowed to elapse before he read it to the National Convention.[2]

This *Rapport sur les trente-deux membres de la Convention détenus en vertu du décret du 2 juin* marks Saint-Just's emergence into the field of practical politics. For the

---

[1] *Archives parlementaires*, LXVIII, 154, note 3.

[2] F. A. Aulard, *Recueil des actes du comité de salut public*, IV, 578 (June 16); V, 2 (June 19); V, 148 (July 2).

first time the young theorist had an opportunity to grapple with actualities, and the result, it must be admitted, was an achievement of dubious merit. His information was inaccurate and incomplete. Only twenty-nine Girondists had been decreed under arrest on June 2, not thirty-two.[1] Of these, he proposed, when he read the report to the Convention on July 8, that some half-a-dozen or so should be declared traitors to the fatherland; he cited three or four names, and included the remainder with a vague *et cetera*.[2] A murmur of anger and apprehension rose from the thinned ranks of the Right, whereupon Saint-Just explained that the decree was aimed only at those who had fled while under arrest. In the version of his discourse printed a few days later by order of the Convention, nine deputies were declared 'traitors to the fatherland' under this indictment, the nine fugitives, Barbaroux, Bergoeing, Birotteau, Buzot, Gorsas, Lanjuinais, Louvet, Pétion and Salle. Yet ten other prisoners had escaped in the same fashion, four of them certainly before June 24 when Saint-Just prepared the first draft of his report. It is difficult to explain his ignorance of these developments. Brissot he omitted entirely from his summary, yet Brissot was one of the original Twenty-nine; he had fled on the 3d of June, had been arrested the 10th at Moulins, and condemned to the Revolutionary Tribunal June 23 by a special decree of the Convention. Possibly Saint-Just felt that Brissot's case, having been made the subject of an explicit decree, was outside the compass of his report; yet he included Barbaroux in his list of 'traitors to the fatherland,' and Barbaroux had likewise been condemned by the Convention in a special vote on June 17.

The desire of the Committee was to avoid as far as possible the appearance of a wholesale proscription. In

---

[1] Claude Perroud, *La proscription des Girondins* (Paris, 1917), pp. 38-39.

[2] *Archives parlementaires*, LXVIII, 436. The complete report is printed here, pp. 426-36; and also in O.C., II, 1-31.

addition to the nine deputies whom Saint-Just designated as traitors, five others only — Gardien, Gensonné, Guadet, Mollevaut and Vergniaud — were to be placed on trial to answer the charge of complicity. The accusations against the remainder were to be dropped. 'All the prisoners are not guilty,' Saint-Just insisted, 'by far the larger number of them were merely misled.' [1] To dissent from the opinion of the majority was no crime; but to take up arms against the National Convention was unpardonable. Some of the fugitives had unquestionably taken up arms, but they had done so after an unjust and arbitrary arrest, and their act might easily be mistaken for self-defense by the uncritical observer. Saint-Just was therefore under the necessity of proving the accused deputies conspirators of old standing, and this attempt led him to cloud the good sense of his report with a list of charges utterly preposterous and unfounded.

For there was nothing in the parliamentary record of the Girondists to prove them less ardent republicans or less devoted patriots than the Jacobins. This fact in itself appeared suspicious to Saint-Just. 'They were never courageous foes of liberty,' he confessed. 'They spoke its language, they posed as its champions. Thus two opposing armies fought under the Roman Eagle.' Seeking to condense this paradoxical situation into an epigram, he flung off one of those dark truths that recoil with such deadly accuracy upon his own head: '*Nothing so nearly resembles virtue as a great crime.*' [2] In their hearts, he proclaimed, the Girondist leaders had been scheming from the first to undo the Revolution, but only the virtuous Montagnards had sensed the perfidy of these designs. The conspirators had fought to save the king, that was well known. But secretly they had been connected with every counter-revolutionary movement, had plotted to place the Duke of York on the French throne, then the Duke of Orleans, and

[1] O.C., II, 4.   [2] O.C., II, 4.

then the son of Louis XVI. They had formed projects to assassinate a part of the National Convention, to foment revolts in the provinces, to plunge France into civil war and to overturn the Republic.

The thunderous exaggeration of these indictments lent to Saint-Just's closing recommendations the air of a lame and impotent conclusion. As spokesman of the Committee, he proposed an amnesty for all but fourteen of the accused, a decision of statesmanlike clemency which the Montagnards refused to share. They voted to adjourn the proposed amnesty until further deliberation, and showed their temper still more clearly by decreeing the arrest of Condorcet and Devérité. Attendance at the Convention, it must be remembered, had fallen in June, 1793, to less than half, sometimes to less than a quarter, of the nominal strength of 750 deputies, while those who did attend were most of them Jacobins.[1] It is not surprising, therefore, that on July 8 this 'Rump' parliament was in a less clement mood than the Committee of Public Safety. The fact helps to explain the changes in the personnel of the Committee which occurred two days later.

Danton appears to have viewed with indifference the waning prestige of his cabinet. One of those fits of lethargy which puzzle his biographers weighed down his spirits in those early days of July. His hopes of uniting the Convention in the prosecution of the foreign war had vanished with the proscription of the Girondists; and he pressed against the rebels of the Vendée the sort of half-hearted measures (he hated civil war) that invited failure. On July 4, and again on July 8, the policies of the Committee were severely criticized, but he made no effort to defend them either in the Convention or at the Jacobin Club. On the 10th word reached Paris that General Westerman had allowed his army to be surprised and badly mangled by the Vendéeans. Camille Desmoulins laid the blame

[1] Perroud, *op. cit.*, pp. 55-57.

upon the Committee of Public Safety, and accused it, in addition, of assuming dictatorial powers. The deputies were in a mood to agree. As the date had arrived for the monthly renewal of the Committee, they decreed that it should be completely reconstructed, and its powers reduced to the limits prescribed on the day of its inception. Danton was not reëlected.

This downfall of the Danton Cabinet suggests a lesson of the highest importance. It had failed, first, because it lacked a skilful and vigorous military director, secondly, because it had lost the confidence of the Convention. These two factors, therefore, might be counted upon to decide the fate of its successor. As the revolutionary enthusiasm precluded all concessions to the enemy, an executive committee could save France only by organizing a victorious army. To do this, it would have to enjoy an indefinite lease of power and exercise a practical dictatorship.

As first created, on April 6, 1793, the Committee of Public Safety had included nine members, but by July successive additions had raised this number to eighteen. The decrees of July 10 reduced it to the original size, reelected seven members — Barère, Couthon, Gasparin, Hérault-Séchelles, Jeanbon-Saint-André, Robert Lindet and Saint-Just — and added two new members, Prieur (de la Marne) and Thuriot. But the changes were not yet complete. On July 27, Robespierre, having an assured majority in the new committee, entered it himself, replacing Gasparin. The need for associates with some military experience led Barère, in the middle of August, to recommend the inclusion of two engineering officers, Lazare Carnot and Prieur (de la Côte d'Or). Thuriot resigned a few weeks later, but about the same time, for reasons of policy, the Committee coöpted Collot d'Herbois and Billaud-Varennes.

With the inclusion of these two terrorists the Great

Committee was complete. It numbered twelve deputies in all — Barère, Couthon, Hérault-Séchelles, Jeanbon-Saint-André, Robert Lindet, Saint-Just, Prieur (de la Marne), Robespierre, Carnot, Prieur (de la Côte d'Or), Collot d'Herbois and Billaud-Varennes in the order of their election. But during the year that the Great Committee functioned, Jeanbon-Saint-André and Prieur (de la Marne) were away on missions almost continuously, and it is the remaining ten, therefore, who deserve to be styled the decemvirs.

They were a curious group. Carnot, Lindet and Prieur (de la Côte d'Or) soon buried themselves in a mass of statistics and correspondence, supervising the supplies and forging the armies for that organization of victory which was to dazzle Europe. Lazare Carnot was the genius of the Committee. Almost alone, he remained unaffected by the psychic derangement of the Terror, the bombast, the attitudinizing and the hysteria. While the Jacobins ranted and thundered, while the Revolutionary Tribunal despatched its *fournées* and the knife of the guillotine rose and fell on the Place de la Révolution, this cool, methodical, tireless man, buried in his bureaux and half-ignored by his colleagues, organized the victories that first saved the Committee and then destroyed it. For by freeing France from invasion Carnot ended the only excuse that could justify the régime of Terror, and when Robespierre sought to prolong the Terror after the need for it had passed, Carnot's victories pursued him, as Barère was to confess, 'like avenging furies.'

It has become a tradition to distinguish between the 'workers' on the Committee and the 'politicians.' This classification is useful, but it must not be accepted as entirely definitive, for all the members laboured incessantly, and there was no rigid apportionment of duties. Billaud-Varennes, Collot d'Herbois and Couthon had charge of the correspondence with the representatives on mission and with the local authorities. Saint-Just was concerned chiefly with constitutional legislation; Saint-André with the Department of Marine; Carnot with the personnel and movements of the armies; Prieur (de la Côte d'Or) with the manufacture of arms and munitions; Lindet with transportation and subsistences; and Barère and Hérault with foreign affairs. Robespierre, although he dabbled in almost everything, remained a minister without portfolio.

What chiefly distinguished the 'politicians,' particularly Robespierre, Couthon, Saint-Just and Barère, was the success with which they defended the Committee of Public Safety in the Convention. Their eloquence wrung from the deputies each month the vote of confidence that renewed the powers of the Committee. On more than one occasion, Robespierre's extraordinary reputation was the particular shield that sheltered the decemvirs from the attacks of the opposition, for the presence of the Incorruptible guaranteed the purity of the government. If the first Committee of Public Safety could fairly be termed a Danton Cabinet, the second, though with less reason, came to be viewed in France and in Europe as the Committee of Robespierre. Yet Robespierre had few of the qualities required in a leader of men. He had little genius for organization; he judged his subordinates by their virtue rather than their ability; and his tender vanity made him a difficult colleague. In reality, he never dominated the Committee to the extent generally credited, and after the first few months his influence over his fellow members began to wane. But so long as his popular prestige endured, it lent an undue weight to his lightest counsels.

Within the Committee, Robespierre's closest confidants were Couthon and Saint-Just. Georges Auguste Couthon was a lawyer from Clermont-Ferrand, an invalid crippled in both legs by pachymeningitis of the dorso-lumbar region. In the Legislative Assembly he had been a

Girondist, but he transferred his allegiance to the Jacobins with the opening of the Convention, and the pressure of events converted him into a terrorist.[1] This gentle-voiced invalid lived in constant agitation, conjuring up in his fevered mind ever new and more fantastic plots against the Republic. In periods of particular stress he pushed his wheel chair tirelessly back and forth between the Committee and the Convention, until his pain-racked body took its revenge and confined him to his bed for days of recuperation. But his brain never rested, and his legal subtlety, which had earned him a share in drafting the Constitution of the Year I, helped him to clothe the most sanguinary decrees of the Committee with a semblance of decency and order. In this service he wore out his energies and aggravated his illness, but his only recorded regret was that he had but half a life to give for his country.

With Robespierre and Couthon, Saint-Just discovered similarities of thought and temperament that drew the three together. All the members of the Committee found it advisible from the first to conserve before the world an appearance of complete friendliness and harmony; but in private debate personal differences asserted themselves. The triumvirs, as Robespierre, Couthon and Saint-Just were later to be termed, looked with an unfriendly eye upon the two 'men of September,' Collot d'Herbois and Billaud-Varennes. Collot, to use Barère's curt phrases, was 'a boor of unparalleled violence'; and Billaud 'a phlegmatic yet irritable individual who never spoke except sententiously or insultingly.'[2] The vulgarity of these two, and their doubtful morals, provoked in Robespierre a fastidious distaste which the passing months hardened into suspicion and contempt.

[1] Geoffrey Bruun, 'The Evolution of a Terrorist: Georges Auguste Couthon,' *Journal of Modern History*, II, No. 3 (September, 1930), pp. 410-29.
[2] Barère, *Mémoires*, I, 195.

To the tactful Barère fell the task of mediating between the groups. Some historians have seen in Bertrand Barère the most contemptible figure in the gallery of the Revolution. The judgment is too harsh. He had imagination and a gift of fervent eloquence; much sagacity, more suppleness, and a complete absence of principles. Under the Old Régime he 'had wished to pass as a gentleman';[1] under the new, his abilities carried him into the Committee of Public Safety. A fellow deputy has left a shrewd description of this astute compromiser. 'Wit, finesse, an eloquence that owed more to the grace than the solidity of the thought; the art of distracting attention; the art of distorting facts and of presenting them under the most favourable aspect; the art still more important of yielding to the turn of circumstances: such was his talent.'[2] This is the opinion of a political foe; but it is true that Barère, a time-server in Danton's Cabinet, passed over to the Montagnard group gracefully after the fall of the Gironde. When Danton fell, he was again ready to sail with the wind, and hastened to place his undoubted talents at the disposal of the triumphant Jacobins. As a reward he remained in the Committee after its reconstruction.

On the fringe of the Committee hung the handsome figure of Hérault-Séchelles, the famous *rédacteur* of the Constitution of the Year I, but a dubious individual, an ex-noble, whose questionable negotiations with the Allied Powers were to bring him to the guillotine within eight months. At the opening of the States General Hérault was a brilliant and debonair *avocat* in the *Parlement de Paris*, but 'Philosophy had thrown him into the Revolution, pride had kept him there, and fear had enchained him.'[3] As a relative of the Polignacs, he would

[1] Joachim Vilate, *Causes secrètes de la journée du 9 au 10 thermidor an 2*, ed. M. Lescure (Paris, 1875), p. 224.

[2] Arnaud Meillan, *Mémoires*, ed. by Berville and Barrière (Paris, 1823), p. 6.

[3] *Recollections of Baron de Frénilly*, ed. by Arthur Chuquet (New York, 1909), p. 124.

have been wiser to emigrate. Blue blood was not easily forgiven in 1793.

The quarters assigned to the Committee of Public Safety were in the *Pavillon de Flore*, a wing of the Palace of the Tuileries, which extended towards the Seine at the point where the Pont Royal crossed it, and which joined the Palace to the terminus of the *Grande Galerie du Louvre*.[1] There, in the 'Green Room' on the ground floor, the decemvirs were to hammer out the destinies of France in grim and secret sessions. Through the summer of 1793, and the winter that followed, a stream of couriers came and went before the entrance, bringing bags of longhand despatches that were soon buried in the undigested litter on the tables. The new masters of France, feverish men with tired eyes, toiled endlessly over this verbose and illegible correspondence. 'The ministry,' Saint-Just groaned, 'is a world of paper.... It is impossible to govern without laconism.'[2] At any point the labours of the Committee were likely to be interrupted by a new emergency — an urgent message from the Convention, perhaps, which would send two or three of the decemvirs hastening past the façade of the Tuileries and across the Palace gardens to the *Salle de Manège*. With patient reproaches or veiled threats they would check an incipient revolt of the Opposition, and then hasten back to the Green Room to their grim discussions and unfinished tasks. When exhaustion overtook them, they flung themselves upon a couch in one of the anterooms to snatch some minutes' sleep, for in times of crisis night could set no period to their labours, and throughout the hours of darkness the fiercely burning candles would blaze down upon the bent heads of men who were burning themselves out no less fiercely.

[1] A. Berty and H. Legrand, *Histoire générale de Paris, Topographie historique du vieux Paris*, II (Paris, 1868), 91.
[2] O.C., II, 87.

CHAPTER VII
PRECARIOUS TENURE

Le gouvernement provisoire de la France est révolutionnaire jusqu'à la paix.
SAINT-JUST, October 10, 1793.[1]

DESPITE the defiant orators of the Mountain, the situation which faced the Great Committee in the mid-summer of 1793 was desperate beyond belief. In the Western Departments revolt burned fiercely, fanned by Buzot, Barbaroux, Guadet, and other fugitive Girondists. In the South, Lyons, Marseilles and Toulon had risen against the Jacobin dictatorship. In the North, the allied armies, with leisurely assurance, were battering down the frontier fortresses. Condé surrendered July 10; Valenciennes the 28th. Maubeuge alone stood between Coburg and Paris.

To organize France, crush the internal revolts and block the foreign invasion, and at the same time consolidate their anomalous authority, was the task that faced the decemvirs. They were condemned to act, and to act immediately, with the most drastic vigour, yet their powers were so limited and their position so irregular that every resolute measure they took squinted at usurpation. Only success could justify the despotic use they were compelled to make of their mandate. To a jealous Convention they insisted at all times that they were the responsible instruments of its will; they declined to assume the title 'Committee of Execution,' preferring the fact to the name, and posed instead as a 'Committee of Surveillance.' The executive functions of government were still to be exercised, nominally at least, by the Provisory Executive Council.

From the outset the Committee found its supremacy

[1] O.C., II, 88.

threatened by opponents eager to profit by the least mis-
play. On August 1, Danton, whose energy had returned
with his defeat, proposed that the Executive Council
should be suppressed altogether, and the Committee of
Public Safety erected into a provisory government with an
appropriation of fifty million francs for expenses. The
decemvirs dared not accept: 'We shuddered,' Saint-Just
declaimed later, 'before a snare so perfidious.'[1] It seemed
too evident that Danton, wiser for his own experience,
proposed to take his revenge by crushing them beneath an
excess of responsibility. Barère, Saint-André and Robespierre therefore repudiated with unanimity and vigour
the proposal to extend the powers of the Committee.
Necessity compelled them, however, to accept the vote of
fifty million francs.[2]

The next manœuvre which the Committee was called
upon to face was a direct one, and far more serious. Early
in September the news spread that Toulon had opened its
gates to the English, and two weeks later it became known
that the Army of the North, despite a partial success at
Hondschoote, had again fallen into a perilous situation.
Mutterings of dissatisfaction filled the Convention. On
September 25 the management of the armies was pointedly
criticized; and when one deputy declared that the blame
for the reverses must rest upon the rascals in office, the
Assembly applauded. For the decemvirs to ignore this
censure was to invite the fate of the Danton Cabinet; to
accept the adjournment perfidiously suggested would have
been to give the agitators time to organize. Though caught
unprepared, the Committee sent its most persuasive members into the breach to meet the attack.

'The discussion you have just heard,' proclaimed Billaud-Varennes, leaping up the steps to the tribune, 'is, I
dare to affirm, the greatest of triumphs for the enemies of

[1] O.C., II, 326. Barère, *Mémoires*, II, 355 f.
[2] *Moniteur*, August 2, 1793.

the Republic. Your Committee of Public Safety has been shuddering, these two days past, at the horrible coalition formed by all the factions which aspire to overthrow the Republic and destroy the National Convention. It is necessary to tear away the veil....' [1] Billaud had formulated the argument for the defense: to the end it never varied. All opposition to the governing committees was sedition, and any deputies bold enough to criticize the running of the machine they had created were malcontents and conspirators. Yet it was by prestige as much as by terror that the Committee kept its power. Billaud scarcely exaggerated when he declared that the overthrow of the Committee would mean the downfall of the Republic. For the tireless and resolute group on the ground floor of the *Pavillon de Flore* were saving France, organizing from the *débris* of ancient institutions an efficient government and a formidable defense. A majority of the deputies in the Convention recognized this. Hating the tyranny of the decemvirs, they felt obliged to support them, for the Committee constituted the only government capable of wresting victory from the national chaos.

Under these circumstances, to oppose the Committee, even from humane and patriotic motives, was to play the enemy's game. This argument, which Billaud proclaimed from the tribune on September 25 with such vehement ardour, Barère sustained with softer phrases. He justified the measures taken by the Committee, painted confidently its achievements, and shifted the blame for the military mishaps in the North to the shoulders of the unfortunate General Houchard. Barère's defense was adroit and disarming, and the Convention applauded when he withdrew.

It was, however, the prestige of Robespierre that reversed the fortunes of the day. In his slow, pedantic sentences, separated by interminable pauses that should

[1] Buchez and Roux, *Histoire parlementaire*, XXIX, 128.

have been ludicrous and were instead somehow impressive, the Incorruptible rebuked his fellow deputies for their want of faith. The spell of Robespierre's oratory is lost and no quotation can revive it. 'What has come over us,' exclaimed one repentant deputy at the close of the sitting, 'when Robespierre has to justify himself before the Mountain?' The Convention affirmed its confidence in the measures of its Committee of Public Safety by a unanimous vote.[1]

In this rhetorical triumph won by his colleagues on September 25, Saint-Just took no part, for it was never his habit to mount the tribune without adequate preparation. His activities during these first precarious weeks in the life of the new Committee are not easy to trace, though it is clear that he remained in Paris throughout the summer. The minutes of the Committee record him as present daily at the sessions in the *Pavillon de Flore*, and the extant decrees bearing his signature show that he was interested chiefly in military affairs. He collected data on the republican armies, their equipment and morale, and held himself in readiness to leave at a moment's notice for any threatened front. On July 18 he was ordered to visit the Departments of the Aisne, the Oise and the Somme, as a Representative-on-mission, but he did not leave, and after several days the assignment was relegated to others. Early in September he wrote his friend Thullier in Blérancourt, 'I am to start within a day or two for the armies,'[2] but again his expectations were deferred, and it was not until the end of October that he actually undertook a mission.

It would seem that sudden fame had added a new note of austerity to Saint-Just's character, for he was too young to wear with ease the consciousness of his grave responsibility. To impress those who approached him, he af-

[1] Buchez and Roux, *op. cit.*, XXIX, 147.
[2] O.C., II, 63.

fected a frigid manner and a habit of clipped incisive speech, and when he walked abroad he wrapped himself in a mantle of gloomy and concentrated thought as befitted a legislator to whom the nation had confided its destinies. The pose was in great part, no doubt, an armour for his inexperience. Petitioners constantly besieged him, to seek places for their friends or to beg his intercession, and this pressure so annoyed him he thought of proposing to the Convention that all public posts should be filled by election. His official manner and the studied laconism with which he delivered his opinions sometimes amused his colleagues. 'You are nothing but a box of aphorisms,' Collot d'Herbois told him one day to his face, for Collot the ex-comedian knew something of acting himself.[1] Camille Desmoulins, who remembered Saint-Just as the obscure youth who had come to Paris in 1789 with the manuscript of his first poem, found the austere manners of the decemvir more than a little irritating. 'One gathers from his bearing,' Camille wrote, 'that he considers his head the corner stone of the Republic, and he carries it on his shoulders with reverence as if it were the Holy Sacrament.'[2] Saint-Just writhed at the satire, and remembered it, but the full flavour of these thrusts may have escaped him. He had no sense of humour.

The official adoption of the Constitution in July, 1793, had robbed the National Convention of its *raison d'être*. Demands for a new Assembly had begun to stir the nation, demands to which the deputies had no intention of yielding, and the Committee decided it would be best to put an end to such agitation by the proclamation of a decree that would legitimatize the existing régime. When the powers of the decemvirs expired on October 10, they sent Saint-Just before the Convention with a proposal that

[1] Sainte-Beuve, *Causeries de lundi*, V, 277.
[2] Camille Desmoulins, *Réponse de Camille Desmoulins à Arthur Dillon* (Paris, 1793), p. 52.

the revolutionary government should be maintained in full force until peace could be achieved.

'In the circumstances in which the Republic finds itself,' Saint-Just stated, 'the Constitution can not be inaugurated; it would destroy itself.'[1] He proposed that the Council, the civil administration, and the armies, should be placed under the surveillance of the Committee of Public Safety, which would report each week to the Convention. The revolutionary government so constituted was then to be proclaimed as permanent until the conclusion of the war. If to a modern reader the implications of the proposed measure seem a little obscure, they were clear enough to the deputies at the time. By accepting the project of the Committee they were given the chance to extend their tenure of office for an indefinite period, and this they proceeded to do with loud applause. At the thought of the increased powers which the decree bestowed upon the Committee of Public Safety they were less enthusiastic, but they decided, on the motion of a single deputy, to continue it unchanged for the ensuing month.[2]

Though its legal status and its usurpations were legitimatized to some extent by this decree, only a genuine military success could render the position of the Committee less than precarious. This was the consideration which persuaded Carnot to risk an action a few days after Saint-Just's appearance at the tribune. The fact that the French armies had survived the summer at all must be attributed to the sloth and bickering of the Allied Powers and the incapacity of their generals. At any time a vigorous offensive on the Scarpe or the Meuse would have routed the disorganized forces of the Republic. But Coburg, unwilling to advance on Paris while Condé, Valenciennes and Maubeuge remained unconquered in his rear, wasted the summer in besieging these positions. The

[1] O.C., II, 83.
[2] *Archives parlementaires*, LXXVI, 318.

morale of the Army of the North had been badly shaken by Dumouriez' desertion. A new leader, Dampierre, was killed in an unsuccessful effort to relieve Condé. Custine, whose army was for the moment safe, with its left wing resting on the Vosges Mountains and its right upon the Rhine — the famous lines of Wissembourg — was called to the Army of the North. But he could do nothing and his failure cost him his head. Meanwhile the garrisons of the beleaguered fortresses were starving. Condé and Valenciennes surrendered in July, and Coburg concentrated his forces for a final thrust.

The new Committee, although it stiffened the resistance of the French forces, was unable to avert further misfortunes. The Army of the North, manœuvring awkwardly towards the relief of Maubeuge, was thrown rudely back across the Scarpe early in August, and a few weeks later Toulon surrendered to the English fleet. The prospect was black, but the Allies proved themselves the unintentional saviours of France. The English and Austrian forces in the Netherlands, instead of coöperating, were split into two sections so that the Duke of York might seize Dunkirk for England. At the same time, Brunswick and Wurmser were prevented from forcing the French lines on the Rhine because of the indecision of the Prussian and Austrian governments. Thus the summer drew to a close with the French armies demoralized but still intact.

The separation of the English and Allied forces in the Low Countries afforded the French an opportunity of which Carnot, newly in charge of military operations, took prompt advantage. The 35,000 men under the command of the Duke of York had no sooner commenced the investment of Dunkirk than they were driven out with heavy losses by a French army under Houchard. The latter failed to make the most of his advantage, however, and the decemvirs, disappointed at his mediocre success when they desperately required the *éclat* of a victory, sent him to the Revolutionary Tribunal. Those were critical days for the Committee, attacked in the Convention and weighed down with a heritage of defeat. Its overthrow would have been almost a certainty had October failed to bring better tidings. On the 8th of that month Lyons was reconquered by the forces of the Convention, and a few days later the Vendéeans were defeated at Cholet. At the same time, Carnot was swiftly and secretly concentrating an army of 60,000 men for the relief of Maubeuge. Joining Jourdan in command of it, he smashed his forces through to the plateau at Wattignies, enfiladed Coburg's lines, and compelled him to raise the siege on October 16.

For the moment Paris was safe, and so, for the moment, was the Committee of Public Safety. But there could be no real respite for the decemvirs. 'Those who make revolutions in the world,' Saint-Just observed significantly, 'those who wish to win to better things, must not sleep except in the tomb.' [1] It was a timely warning, for the same week which saw the French armies successful at Wattignies found them asleep on the Rhine. To save Maubeuge, Carnot had drawn 30,000 men from the forces of the Rhine and Moselle. A sudden drive in mid-October broke the depleted lines in this sector and separated the two armies, that of the Rhine being left in a critical position. Landau, the key to the Wissembourg lines, was speedily surrounded, and Strasbourg was threatened. One more effort, apparently, would establish the Austrians in Alsace for the winter; the Prussians might then take up their quarters in Lorraine, and the two armies would be in a position to sweep across France in the spring.

[1] O.C., II, 84.

CHAPTER VIII
THE PROCONSUL OF TERROR

On fait trop de lois, trop peu d'exemples.
SAINT-JUST TO ROBESPIERRE, December 14, 1793.[1]

THE Committee of Public Safety faced the new danger which threatened the Army of the Rhine with promptness and energy. On October 17 two special representatives were ordered to Alsace, 'with full authority to originate such measures for the public safety as they might judge expedient.' The importance attached to their mission is evident from the wording of the decree which granted them not merely the *pouvoirs illimités* usually ascribed to representatives-on-mission, but *pouvoirs extraordinaires*. The men chosen for this duty and entrusted with these illimitable responsibilities were two youths still in their twenties, Saint-Just and Philippe Le Bas.[2]

Le Bas was a modest and generous youth who was guided by a spirit of fervent patriotism and a deep admiration for Robespierre. He had married, in the summer of 1793, the daughter of Robespierre's landlord, and was grieved at the prospect of forsaking his young wife. Saint-Just therefore consented to let Madam Le Bas and her sister Henriette accompany them to Alsace, and the four travelled as far as Saverne in the same carriage. To the close of her life, Madame Le Bas retained a clear memory of Saint-Just's attentions to herself and her sister during the journey. He had stipulated that they should not discuss political matters, but as the carriage rolled through the autumn countryside he chatted

[1] O.C., II, 161.
[2] Aulard, *Recueil des actes du comité de salut public*, VII, 464; *Archives parlementaires*, LXXVII, 429–30.

pleasantly of other subjects, showing the passengers the most delicate attentions and the thoughtfulness of an affectionate brother. To pass the hours he and Le Bas took turns in reading aloud from the plays of Molière and the tales of Rabelais.[1]

At Saverne the ladies were left behind at headquarters, while the two representatives hastened to the point of danger. Two main factors, they discovered, had provoked the disaster which had overtaken the Armies of the Rhine and the Moselle. On August 8 the Committee of Public Safety had withdrawn approximately one-third of the forces from the Rhine to support operations in Belgium, and the 60,000 soldiers remaining were insufficient to hold a line which extended from Strasbourg along the Sarre to the Moselle.[2] A second factor was the disorganization of the staff caused by the policy of 'republicanizing' the army. Buchotte, the Minister of War, and an ardent Jacobin, had cashiered as untrustworthy a number of officers whose commissions dated from the days of the monarchy. The republican armies were not a friendly place for an officer who was also a gentleman, and retirement, demotion and desertion had decimated the ranks. The morale and discipline of the troops had suffered severely from this purging, and new officers could not be trained quickly enough to fill the gaps.

Saint-Just and Le Bas undertook to restore order by swift and vigorous decrees which electrified the forces. 'It was time that Saint-Just visited this unlucky army,' wrote an admirer from Strasbourg. 'He has vivified, reanimated, regenerated everything.... The collection of his decrees will form, beyond dispute, one of the most

[1] Stéfane-Pol, 'Autour de Robespierre: Le conventionnel Le Bas,' *La nouvelle revue* (November, 1900), N.S. 7, pp. 77–106.

[2] Aulard, *Recueil des actes du comité de salut public,* V, 507; Chuquet, Arthur, *Wissembourg,* p. 73 f.; Charavay, Etienne, 'Le général Carlenc,' *Bulletin historique et philologique du comité des travaux historiques et scientifiques* (Paris, 1896), pp. 523–54.

glorious historical monuments of the Revolution.'[1] The impetuous energy of Saint-Just's proclamations has moved some eulogists to rank them with the stirring orders of the youthful Bonaparte. They have the same force and brevity, it is true, but they nowhere attain the intimate magic of the Napoleonic touch. The first one he issued will serve as an example.

The Representatives of the People, on special mission to the Army of the Rhine, to the soldiers of that Army.

We have arrived, and we swear in the name of the Army that the enemy will be vanquished. If there are among you any who are traitors to the cause of the people, we are armed with powers to strike them down. Soldiers, we have come to avenge you, and to give you leaders who will marshal you to victory. We have resolved to seek out, to reward, and to promote the deserving; and to track down all the guilty, whoever they may be. Courage, brave Army of the Rhine! Henceforward you will be happy in the triumph of liberty — happy and victorious!

All commanders, officers, and agents of the government are hereby ordered to satisfy within three days the just grievances of the soldiers. After that interval we will ourselves hear any complaints, and we will offer such examples of justice and severity as the Army has not yet witnessed.

SAINT-JUST   LE BAS[2]

The promise of new and vigorous measures of discipline was no idle threat. Saint-Just and Le Bas proved it by organizing a military tribunal for the Army of the Rhine, erected in accordance with the decree of the National Convention dating from the previous May. So many exaggerated ideas still persist concerning the injustice and ferocity of the Revolutionary Courts that it is necessary to analyse the work of this Commission created by the order of Saint-Just. It is to be borne in mind that a military

[1] Charles Vellay, 'Un ami de Saint-Just: Gateau,' *Annales révolutionnaires*, I (1908), 72.
[2] O.C., II, 108.

tribunal, functioning on the frontier of an invaded country, cannot be expected to observe all the legal niceties of a civil court.

A decree of the National Convention, dated May 12, 1793, directed that two military tribunals were to be established with each army. They were to consist of three judges and a prosecutor, all chosen by the Executive Council and ratified by the Committee of Public Safety. Accusations were first to be considered by the military police, then, if the evidence in support of them appeared sufficient, were to be reported to the military prosecutor, who convoked the Military Tribunal. A list of eighteen names, comprising officers and men, was submitted to the accused man, who selected nine to constitute his jury. The trial was public; the Secretary of the Court read the act of accusation, witnesses were called, and the accused had the right to criticize the testimony and to speak on his own behalf. One of the three judges, acting as President of the Court, then summed up the evidence, and the jury deliberated in secret before rendering a verdict. Each juror submitted his decision individually, and, if he voted 'Guilty,' might add, 'With extenuating circumstances.' A two-thirds vote sufficed for either conviction or acquittal, and the sentence went into effect within twenty-four hours.[1]

In the first four months of its existence the Tribunal of the first military district of the Army of the Rhine tried 660 cases. Of the accused, 282 were acquitted; 316 received sentences ranging from removal to the interior to imprisonment with irons; and 62 were condemned to death. Crimes such as theft and pillage were rigorously punished, whereas breaches of discipline and even insubordination on the part of the soldiers often earned only nominal sentences. The Court showed itself lenient

[1] Georges Michon, 'La justice militaire sous la Révolution,' *Annales révolutionnaires*, XIV (1922), 99–130.

towards the rank and file, and harsh towards the officers, especially towards any found guilty of negligence or cowardice.[1]

The civil population of Alsace was also subjected to the rigours of military law. The belief that the French reverses were the result of enemy intrigues led the representatives to issue orders for domiciliary visits and the arrest of all suspected persons. Some forty of the civic officials were also arrested on the charge of conspiring to deliver up the city. There was a legitimate basis for this fear of intrigues, but the repressive measures were unnecessarily severe. Saint-Just and Le Bas did not intervene in the prosecutions, they only supervised the legal machinery. Their mission, it is fair to add, was unmarked by any act of personal despotism, and no punishments were inflicted save by the due process of the law, such as it was. But because they embodied the spirit of the Terror they have been pictured as monsters of unbridled ferocity. In reality they wielded the Terror methodically, using it as both a curb and a stimulus, with a political sagacity that put to shame the excesses of many of their older colleagues.

The restoration of discipline in the Armies of the Rhine and the Moselle had to be pressed, in order that offensive movements might be undertaken before winter had made the roads impassable. Carnot planned to concentrate the Army of the Moselle on the Saar, whence it could strike due eastward and relieve Landau. The Army of the Rhine, held to its position by the pressure around Strasbourg, was to keep the main Austro-Prussian force engaged there until the Army of the Moselle, having secured Landau, could turn south into the Rhine valley, threatening the enemy's flank and rear. Such a plan was in keeping with Carnot's usual strategy. The extraordinary mobility developed by the French infantry favoured his practice of a

[1] Michon, *op. cit.*, p. 117 f.

sudden concentration upon a weak point in the opposing lines, to be followed, if the latter were broken, by rapid flanking movements. The manœuvre in this case, if effectively carried out, would, it was hoped, lead to the capture or destruction of a considerable part of the enemy forces; but it demanded a strict adherence to plan, and a close coöperation between the commanders of the two French armies.

Following the wishes of the Committee of Public Safety, Saint-Just and Le Bas persuaded Pichegru to assume the command of the Army of the Rhine, and a few days later the Army of the Moselle was entrusted to the young and ardent Hoche. Both generals devoted the first three weeks of November to the problem of proper organization and discipline. The efforts of Pichegru were ably seconded by Saint-Just and Le Bas, who persuaded the Committee to recall five of the representatives in that sector on the ground that they had become superfluous — 'two energetic representatives are enough for this army,' Saint-Just decided within a few hours of his arrival. This action, coupled with his arrogant manner, earned for Saint-Just the not unnatural enmity of the other representatives, who declined to recognize the extraordinary powers with which he and Le Bas had been invested by the Committee of Public Safety.[1]

By November 17, Hoche considered the Army of the Moselle, which had been increased to some forty thousand men, in a fit condition to advance. He fell upon the Prussians at the moment when the latter were withdrawing to a fortified position which they had prepared as their winter line of defense. Thinking that he had forced the retreat, the youthful general pressed on hotly, and was soon drawn too far to the north to coöperate effectively with Pichegru as originally planned. The Prussians, surprised at the vigour of the assault, determined to fall

[1] O.C., II, 109; Aulard, *Recueil des actes du comité de salut public*, VII, 464.

back still further, upon positions which they knew to be practically impregnable to direct attack, and there to await the impetuous republicans. On November 28, Hoche found the enemy established on the heights of Kaiserslautern, and he threw his columns against them. The twenty thousand Prussians under Brunswick were outnumbered, but their position was eminently defensible and well prepared. After three days of desperate assaults Hoche was forced to retire upon his base. He had lost over two thousand men, and had done little to relieve Landau, which was still holding out stubbornly forty miles to the south.

The jealousy existing between the generals and representatives with the two armies was such that Hoche's reverse did not fail to excite some secret satisfaction at the headquarters of the Army of the Rhine. Saint-Just and Le Bas, foreseeing a time when the command of the two armies would require a closer unification, had decided to propose Pichegru as commander-in-chief. But they took no hasty action, nor did they permit their preference to influence them unduly. Saint-Just wrote Hoche a tactful and considerate letter, commending his energy, and urging the advantages which might yet be gained by a closer co-operation between the generals. The Committee of Public Safety proved equally lenient. 'A reverse is not a crime when one has done all possible to make it a victory,' Carnot wrote Hoche; and in a despatch to the representatives with the Army of the Moselle he added, 'Would it not have been better to have marched more directly on Landau, as the Committee first suggested, instead of inclining so far to the north? But nothing is lost providing Landau holds out. We count upon your courage, dear colleagues, and upon the capacity of the general whom we persist in regarding, despite the check he has received, as worthy of our confidence.' [1]

[1] O.C., II, 152; *Correspondance générale de Carnot*, ed. Etienne Charavay (4 vols., Paris, 1892), IV, 232; Aulard, *Recueil des actes du comité de salut public*, IX, 204.

While the troops were resting after Hoche's misadventure, Saint-Just and Le Bas paid a flying trip to Paris. In accord with their suggestion, the Committee had withdrawn four of the representatives in Alsace, but those remaining continued to deplore the lack of cordiality and cooperation between the two armies, the blame for which they laid to the attitude of Saint-Just and Le Bas. Despite these complaints and calumnies, the Committee ordered the two trouble-makers back to the frontier. Their extraordinary powers over the Army of the Rhine had been extended to include also the Army of the Moselle, and they proposed to appoint Pichegru commander-in-chief at the first favourable moment. The representatives Baudot and Lacoste, their most active critics, were so disgusted at this setback that they demanded their own recall, but as it was not forthcoming they remained with Hoche.[1]

The latter had profited by his defeat. He reorganized his forces, revived the spirits of his men, and prepared to carry out the direct advance on Landau which Carnot had urged. Reinforcements numbering ten thousand men were despatched to him, and he used them to strengthen and extend his right wing to join the Army of the Rhine. The latter army, under the more cautious Pichegru, had been progressing slowly, in the face of natural obstacles and a stubborn resistance. On December 14, the two commanders met for a conference which resulted in a somewhat better understanding, but their mutual jealousy continued to embarrass the operations. A week of heavy fighting followed, until Hoche, on December 22, gained a decided victory that opened the road to Landau. Jubilant at his success, Baudot and Lacoste, without consulting or even informing their colleagues, seized the opportunity to proclaim him commander-in-chief of the two armies, communicating their decision to the Committee on December 24.[2]

[1] Aulard, *Recueil des actes du comité de salut public*, IX, 204, 280, 326, 498, 534.
[2] *Ibid.*, 662.

The chagrin of Saint-Just was intense. Not only had his rivals disregarded his authority, they had out-manœuvred him, for to overrule their action would have confused and divided the armies when victory was beckoning. He therefore confirmed the promotion of Hoche, pending the arrival of further instructions from the Committee of Public Safety. To the latter he composed a despatch couched in terms of restrained bitterness.

In conformity with your intentions, we issued on our return a decree instructing the two generals in command of the Moselle and the Rhine to concert their plans for the relief of Landau without delay. We gave to Pichegru the supervision of the united forces. The two generals held a conference, and the next day the first advance took place. We were anticipating great results from the cordial relations which appeared to exist between the two generals. Hoche was young and ardent. Pichegru more mature and more experienced; his first orders held the promise of a decisive victory. Yesterday we arrived at Hagenau. Pichegru revealed to us a decree of Baudot and Lacoste conferring the rank of commander-in-chief upon Hoche, who had accepted it.

Pichegru also referred to us some orders which Hoche had already issued to him. The situation was a most delicate one. It was essential at that moment to think only of the Nation, to assuage all bitter feeling, to check any discouragement, and to prevent the outbreak of the passions which such a situation might excite. We acted with all prudence. We went to see Hoche. But why, when you send two of your number to supervise the execution of your plans, when you and ourselves together share this great responsibility, why do you abandon the country to the control of those who exercise their power in so hasty and so ill-advised a manner? You must have left them unacquainted with your intentions, or they would not have overridden our orders. But count upon our devotion; it will never permit us to compromise the public interest by any weakness or pride. You know best what you are about.

We trust all will go well. Render justice to Pichegru. He has despatched fifteen thousand of his men to Hoche, and with those remaining he has had to recover the territory lost by the treason at Wissembourg. He created a vigorous diversion while Hoche was attacking with the major forces. Let us know at the earliest moment the decision of the Committee. We will do all we can to maintain harmony. This development must not produce a mis-understanding that might divide and discourage the armies in the midst of their triumph. Remember always to hasten on the supplies.

Salut et fraternité

SAINT-JUST   LE BAS [1]

From this episode may be dated the hostility of certain members of the Committee of Public Safety towards Hoche. 'We learn with annoyance and surprise,' Carnot wrote Baudot and Lacoste, 'that you have subordinated the position of Pichegru as commander of the Army of the Rhine.... Whatever may be the merits of General Hoche, in whom we have great confidence, we did not believe that he would have accepted the post of com-mander-in-chief of the two armies save with great reluc-tance, for the generals appeared to us to be working together with a high degree of coöperation and mutual esteem.' At the same time Robespierre wrote to Saint-Just and Le Bas: 'I am filled with alarm lest, in the midst of success and on the eve of victory, you should be checked by the fatal consequences resulting from what is either an unfortunate complication or a miserable conspiracy.' [2]

As a military measure the promotion of Hoche was justified by immediate results. On December 26, he recom-menced his vigorous attacks. The French troops flung themselves upon the Austrian forces about the village of Altenstadt, and at the same time wrested from them the peak of the Geisberg. Unable to make a stand at any point, the Imperial regiments were completely routed, and only the arrival of the Duke of Brunswick with Prussian

[1] O.C., II, 157-58.

[2] Aulard, *Recueil des actes*, IX, 754: Charavay, *Correspondance générale de Carnot*, IV, 253.

aid saved the remnants of Wurmser's army, and gave him an opportunity to reform his shattered divisions behind the Lauter.

This battle proved decisive in the reconquest of the Wissembourg lines. Two days later the garrison of Landau saw the investing Prussian army in sudden retreat, and opened its gates to the Republicans. The representatives, their enmity laid aside for the moment, united in despatching a message of victory to the Convention. But Hoche, who made little attempt to conceal his opinion of Pichegru's mediocrity, was dissatisfied at the necessity of sharing his credit with the latter, and the jealousy between the generals burned more fiercely than ever. To end it, the Committee of Public Safety confirmed Hoche in command of the Army of the Rhine-and-Moselle, while consoling Pichegru with the command of the Army of the North.

Carnot expected Hoche to pursue the advantages which he had gained in the closing days of the year, and occupy the Palatinate. But the morale of his army had degenerated with victory; cold weather set in; and problems of transportation made a further advance impossible. Such at least was the substance of Hoche's excuses to the Committee. At the end of January, Carnot ordered him to place his troops in winter quarters. 'The opportunity has slipped away,' he wrote Baudot and Lacoste with asperity. 'The enemy has now gathered his strength again and could resist the blow that might so easily have been delivered immediately after the victory.... The armies of the Rhine and Moselle would not now be suffering from lack of supplies if you had operated in the Palatinate in accordance with the orders of the Committee of Public Safety.' [1]

'The Committee,' declared Barère in his *Mémoires*, 'was irritated by the disobedience, the pride, and the

[1] Charavay, *Correspondance générale de Carnot*, IV, 293.

spiteful jealousy of Hoche.'[1] On March 10, he was relieved of his command on the Rhine and ordered to the Army of Italy. The Committee, which had hesitated to arrest him at the head of his army, took him into custody when he reached Nice, and he remained in prison until the fall of Robespierre. Hoche's arrest has been consistently imputed to the malignity of Saint-Just, but the responsibility was in reality more widely distributed. Only the general's successes had justified his growing presumption; when these failed, Carnot, Robespierre, Barère, and Buchotte, the Minister of War, as well as Saint-Just, were agreed that his conduct was unbecoming a republican general. To suppose that Saint-Just alone could have persuaded the Committee to arrest Hoche is to attribute to him an influence that he never possessed.[2]

The early days of January, 1794, found Saint-Just back in Paris. His services on the Rhine had proved his value as a disciplinarian, and revealed powers of organization that the Committee knew how to use. Within two weeks a new mission had been found for him, and on January 22 he was ordered to the Army of the North, where lethargy, confusion and conspiracy were paralyzing operations. He left at once for Lille and Maubeuge, armed with unlimited powers and accompanied by the ever-faithful Le Bas.

It was to be the program of Strasbourg repeated, but somewhat less harshly this time. Orders for the reestablishment of discipline, for compulsory loans and the requisition of supplies followed one another rapidly. 'I have seen our colleagues Saint-Just and Le Bas,' wrote a representative from Lille on February 3. 'They have dis-

---

[1] Barère, *Mémoires*, II, 170.

[2] On the question of Hoche's arrest, see Aulard, *Etudes et leçons sur la Révolution française*, I, 204 ff.; Chuquet, *Hoche et la lutte pour l'Alsace*, p. 232; Edmond Bonnal, *Carnot* (Paris, 1888), p. 179 f.; Henri Wallon, *Les représentants du peuple* (5 vols., Paris, 1889), IV, 215.

covered a counter-revolution in Lille,' he added iron-
ically.[1] At Maubeuge another conspiracy was unearthed,
subsidized by English gold and conceived for the betrayal
of the city. The usual methods were invoked to combat
it: an Englishman found in the city was arrested, the
military commission was spurred to greater activity, and
the popular societies urged to scrutinize rigorously the
acts of all civic officials. In justice to the two austere and
zealous proconsuls of the Terror, it must again be urged
that they sought to direct their severity only where they
conceived it might prove salutary. The rectification of
errors committed by more ferocious subordinates, and the
release of innocent suspects, formed not an inconsiderable
part of their labours.[2]

Unfortunately, in Lille as in Strasbourg, Saint-Just's
imperious spirit antagonized those with whom he shared
his responsibilities. The exercise of unlimited authority
confirmed his natural pride until he found it difficult to
subdue it even in writing his colleagues on the Committee.
A letter which he drew up on January 31 (Le Bas was
never more than a second in these matters) was particularly curt in its criticism of the transport system for which
Lindet and Carnot were in the last analysis responsible.
'The organization of the convoy system,' he wrote, 'is
lacking in common sense. All the wagons start from the
same place; one trunk road is jammed with seven hundred
vehicles, the bread and forage arrive late and the horses
perish. Why not establish the supply depots and stores of
forage at the points from which the armies are to operate?'
On the subject of the spring offensive he lectured the
mature Carnot in the manner of a superior. 'It will be the
wisest course on your part to be the aggressors, to be the
first to open the action; and since your forces will be large,
you can at the same moment launch an army against

[1] Aulard, *Recueil des actes*, X, 652.
[2] Wallon, *Les représentants du peuple*, IV, 210; O.C., II, 188.

Ostende, one against Beaumont, surround Valenciennes and attack the forest of Mormale.' [1]

This letter was written at the close of January. Three months remained to the decemvirs for preparation before spring would loose the armies for a new campaign. During that lull in military operations, Paris became once more the undisputed centre of the revolutionary drama, for the conflict between the Committee of Public Safety and the factions had reached a critical stage. To triumph abroad, the Committee was obliged to crush its opponents at home, and Robespierre, who saw the crisis approaching, called Saint-Just to his support. Willingly enough Saint-Just obeyed the summons. The destiny which had drawn him to Alsace when the fate of the Revolution hung in the balance there now called him to Paris to engage in a campaign no less desperate. He seemed able to follow, as if by instinct, the focal point of the revolutionary activity.

[1] O.C., II, 191.

CHAPTER IX

THE FIGHT WITH THE FACTIONS: THE PRELIMINARIES

*Ces factions, nées avec la Révolution, l'ont suivie dans son cours,
comme les reptiles suivent le cours des torrents.*

SAINT-JUST, March 31, 1794.[1]

In the closing months of 1793, the Jacobin Party, although it dominated the National Convention, and controlled public opinion throughout France, found itself threatened by the conflict of internal factions. The struggle with the Gironde had disciplined and dressed its ranks, but victory slackened the bonds of unity until it grew clearly evident that the party would no longer march with an even front. The Right Wing lost momentum, and a group of deputies in the Convention — some from fear, like Basire and Chabot, some from humanity, like Desmoulins and Philippeaux, some from mixed motives, like Thuriot and Danton — began to urge a relaxation of the Terror. They were consequently stigmatized as *Indulgents*. At the same time, the Left Wing, under the lead of such *sans-culotte* extremists as Hébert and Chaumette, was swinging too far forward, urging egalitarian doctrines and a war to the knife against the aristocrats and the wealthy. Between these two rival factions the Committee of Public Safety steered a tortuous middle course, maintaining itself with skill amid the confusion of a three-cornered fight.

To the decemvirs, the *Indulgents* appeared the more serious menace, because they had a strong following in the Convention. Joining forces with other malcontents, they formed what would have been considered the Party of the

[1] O.C., II, 306.

Opposition in a more normal parliament. Their intrigues against the government were incessant, and each month they aspired to overthrow the Committee by an adverse vote on the renewal of its powers. The story of this monthly manœuvring has already been traced to October, 1793. The skirmishes of November and December, which took place while Saint-Just was absent in Alsace, marked the culmination of this system of attack. The 10th of November, in particular, witnessed the opening of a confused struggle wherein the decemvirs lost their bearings and were frozen with uncertainty. Even Robespierre, sensing conspiracies everywhere about him, was baffled when he tried to guess from which side the blow might be delivered, and from November 10 to November 13 he was like the captain of a fog-bound ship who peers anxiously into a perilous mist.

This three-day crisis in the affairs of the Committee of Public Safety has been obscured too long by the picturesque drama of the *Fête de la Raison*. The extravagant rites which marked the installation of the Goddess of Reason in Nôtre Dame on November 10, 1793, have been supposed to explain Robespierre's resentment against the Hébertist faction, but the explanation is much simpler than the facts. The truth is that at this period the Hébertists and the Committee, instead of being at enmity, were making common cause against the *Indulgents*. When the religious carnival is fitted into the political setting, the centre of interest is found, not in the blasphemy at Nôtre Dame, but in the quiet struggle that was fought out during these same days in the National Convention.

The movement for dechristianization had disturbed the Committee of Public Safety from its inception. During September the idea spread with extraordinary rapidity through Paris and the provinces, receiving a strong stimulus in October from the publication of the new revolutionary calendar. On November 6, Pierre Philippeaux moved that the report of Fabre d'Eglantine on the calendar should be printed and distributed, and Thuriot and Basire urged a campaign of destruction against the Catholic Church. Now these men were not Hébertists, they were *Indulgents*. It was not until several days later that such men as Anacharsis Cloots and Anaxagoras Chaumette joined their voices actively in the cry for dechristianization, and so presented the unusual spectacle of *Indulgents* and *Enragés* chanting in unison. The project excited such enthusiasm that the Paris Commune appointed the 20th Brumaire (November 10) as a civic fête, to mark the end of fanaticism and the installation of the Cult of Liberty and Reason.

As indicated above, the campaign had been opened by such *Indulgents* as Thuriot, Basire and Chabot, which was sufficient to arouse the suspicion of the decemvirs. Thuriot had been an implacable enemy of the Committee of Public Safety since his resignation from it on September 20. When the movement also enlisted the support of the Hébertist faction, such an alliance, even if it were fortuitous, could not fail to disquiet the members of the Committee. Their uneasiness can scarcely have been diminished by the choice of November 10, the day on which their powers would expire, for the installation of the new religion. Popular demonstrations must always alarm an insecure government.

On the day indicated, the *Indulgents* launched a parliamentary campaign against the Committees. The system of the Terror was denounced amid cheers, and Chabot and Basire forced through the Convention a decree securing each deputy against arrest unless he were given a chance to plead his case before his fellow deputies. This move struck the sword from the hands of the decemvirs so far as their enemies in the Assembly were concerned; but none of them, if present at the session, dared to object, nor did they venture, in an atmosphere so unfriendly, to pose the question of their expiring powers. With the policy of the Terror under criticism, and the recent misfortunes in Alsace still unredressed, the decemvirs felt their fortunes at an ebb. Within a day or two at best they knew they would have to risk a vote on the crucial test of their reappointment, and if it failed to carry they would lose the shield of authority and be delivered over to their enemies.

From this predicament they were rescued by the Hébertists. As the most ardent defenders of the Terror, the *Exagérés* construed Chabot's criticism of it as an attack upon themselves, and they retaliated with the full flood of their colourful invective. Hébert's journal, *Le Père Duchesne*, was *en grande colère* against the *Indulgents*, calling them allies of Austria and of Pitt, traitors to the Mountain, rascals who were plundering the Republic. These outbursts reassured the decemvirs and they opened a counter-offensive against their foes in the Convention. Barère had borrowed an Hébertist phrase — 'If the Revolution retrogrades everything is lost' — and the Opposition broke under the attack. On November 12, Chabot's proposal to grant accused deputies a special hearing before the Convention was rescinded, and the Committee took advantage of the favouring sentiment to secure at the same time the renewal of its powers.

Chabot and Basire had defied the lightnings: they were doomed. Their records were anything but unimpeachable, and within a week the Committee of General Security found an excuse to arrest them, to the *grande joie* of the *Père Duchesne*. This bolt, falling suddenly amid their ranks, daunted the deputies of the Opposition, and the Committee of Public Safety marched on with stern resolve. A decree demanding a further extension of powers, and the authority to negotiate with foreign courts, was presented to the intimidated Convention, which voted the decemvirs the added authority with sullen acquiescence

When December 10 brought the question of renewal once more to the fore, the *Indulgents* once more gathered together their forces. Bourdon (de l'Oise) declared that some of the members of the Committee had lost the confidence of the Assembly; Merlin (de Thionville) suggested that it should be renewed by a third each month. But a majority of the deputies sat in uneasy silence, and when the vote was finally taken the prestige of the Committee carried it through by a narrow margin.[1]

The *Indulgents* were checked, but the *Exagérés*, who had been unleashed with such effectiveness at a critical juncture, were not easily muzzled again. Their influence was on the decline, for Carnot was breaking their hold upon the Ministry of War and the Army; but at the Hôtel de Ville their control was still assured so long as they dominated the General Council. On December 1, this Council ordered the revolutionary committees of the sections to report to itself, instead of to the Committee of General Security, a direct act of usurpation which the decemvirs had to block by a hasty restraining order which they rushed through the Convention. The Hébertists required a lesson and Robespierre was prepared to let them have it. On December 17, partly to curb the *Exagérés*, partly to placate the *Indulgents*, the blow was struck. Vincent, secretary to the Minister of War, and Ronsin, Commander of the Revolutionary Army, were arrested and held for investigation.

The Committee of Public Safety was moving with more assurance in its contest with the factions because its own prestige had increased. Its most eloquent advocates were the victories which closed the year. At Le Mans, on December 12, and a few days later at Savenay, the Vendéean insurgents were crushed; while in Alsace, Hoche and Pichegru drove back the Allied forces and relieved Landau. At the same time the Committee was able to announce the

[1] *Archives parlementaires*, LXXIX, 460, note 1; LXXX, 364, 367, and 629.

recapture of Toulon, and the news struck the enemies of the government, as Robespierre noted grimly, 'like a personal defeat.'

After these victories the frontal attacks on the Committee were abandoned. A majority of the deputies in the Convention were convinced that the despotism of the decemvirs, however odious, was at least a guarantee of success. The question of the monthly reappointment of the Committee ceased to be a fighting issue and the vote passed thenceforth without debate. But the Opposition Party was active in other directions. Having failed to unseat the decemvirs by direct attacks, it hurled its forces against the weaker outworks of the government, against the Hébertist faction which was declining but still might play the Committee's game; and against the superfluous ministries, which the decemvirs controlled but for which they accepted no responsibility. So well calculated were these indirect attacks, especially when they seemed most haphazard, that Robespierre came to feel more and more certain that the manœuvres of the Opposition masked a widespread conspiracy to overturn the government and destroy the Revolution. He pledged himself to the task of tracing the hidden roots of the conspiracy, until the whole plot was clear to him and he could denounce it to the Convention.

One deputy, whose pamphlets annoyed the government in the early winter of 1793-94, was Pierre Philippeaux. Sent on a mission to the Vendée in June, he had quarrelled with the generals, and returned to Paris to vindicate his case. After appealing in vain to the Committee, he included it in his denunciations, publishing and distributing among the deputies an account of the horrors he had witnessed in the civil war. He was forthwith denounced at the Jacobin Club, on January 7, as a moderate, along with Camille Desmoulins. Desmoulins, a far more brilliant writer than Philippeaux, had opened an attack on the government in his journal *Le Vieux Cordelier*, in the third and fourth numbers of which he praised 'the courageous Philippeaux' for his revelations of the Vendéean atrocities, and indicted the decemvirs for tyranny under the disguise of translating Tacitus.[1]

An uncensored journal published by a writer as clever and as independent as Desmoulins was a menace which an unpopular government could not ignore. 'If,' boasted Camille, 'the liberty of the press alone survived, in a country where the most absolute despotism had centred all authority in a single hand, it would suffice to right the balance.' Regarding his translations from Tacitus, in which many found allusions of contemporary significance, he declared, 'Those who read in these accurate depictions of tyranny an unfortunate resemblance to their own conduct should hasten the correction of it.'[2] Robespierre was always unduly sensitive to accusations of tyranny, and this last thrust stirred him. 'It is useless to read the fifth number of the *Vieux Cordelier*,' he exhorted the Jacobins. 'Your opinion of Camille ought already to be fixed. You see in his work the most revolutionary principles joined to maxims of the most pernicious moderantism.' He proposed that the journal should be burned. Camille's answer has become historic. 'Very well said, Robespierre,' he affirmed quietly, 'but burning is no answer.'[3]

It is possible to observe a growing acerbity in Robespierre's speeches after the opening of the year 1794. His health was not good, and the continual strife among the factions wearied him. Convinced that the triumph of the Committee was the same thing as the triumph of the Revolution, he came to view opposition to the govern-

[1] Aulard, *Recueil des actes*, V, 58; VII, 285-86; Aulard, *La Société des Jacobins* (6 vols., Paris, 1889-97), V, 595-600. The third and fourth numbers of the *Vieux Cordelier* are reproduced in Buchez et Roux, *Histoire parlementaire*, XXXI, 173-96.

[2] Buchez et Roux, *Histoire parlementaire*, XXXI, 193 and 196.

[3] Aulard, *La Société des Jacobins*, V, 699.

ment as treason. As he penetrated the successive plots by which the leaders of the Opposition sought to harass and overthrow the Committee, he became obsessed with the conviction that in these men he was fighting the allies of Pitt and Coburg and the Comte d'Artois. To justify his belief he had accumulated a pile of evidence, which was small in itself, but became large and terrifying when viewed through the refracting passions of the day. A man whose life depends upon the issue is not likely to draw a very fine distinction between suspicion and proof.

He set his spies to uncover the cause for the ceaseless agitation that stirred the Convention. The most persistent enemy of the Committee, and the most subtle, appeared to be Bourdon (de l'Oise). 'A fool,' Baudot called him, 'forever arriving drunk at the evening sessions.'[1] But Bourdon, or those behind him, showed a clear understanding of the Committee's position, and its vulnerable points. Its practical immunity from attack was the result of its anomalous status. If the Convention could have been persuaded to erect it into a Committee of Government, and to abolish the ministries, no evasion of responsibility would have been possible. Three times during December, Bourdon proposed this measure and Philippeaux supported him. The decemvirs were greedy for power, but they distrusted Greek gifts. Foiled in this project, Bourdon then struck a shrewd and sudden blow in a new quarter. On January 7, 1794, he declared that the ministers were wasting the public revenues, and proposed that no further expenditures should be authorized unless the Committees presented an itemized requisition. Danton supported the proposal, and it was passed by the Convention, but the decemvirs dared to disregard it on the excuse that so much red tape would have held up the army supplies indefinitely.

[1] Marc-Antoine Baudot, *Notes historiques sur la Convention nationale* (Paris, 1893), p. 121.

When the hunting instinct was roused in the Assembly, the decemvirs felt like animals which expect at any moment to find themselves at bay. This sense of common danger bound them together and forced them to defend each other in public. They clung to power because they dared not relinquish it, yet any day might bring an adverse vote of the deputies that would sweep them from office. Robespierre had no illusions about the probable sequence. If once the enemies of the Committee won the upper hand, they could, as he trenchantly expressed it, 'proscribe at will the defenders of Liberty whom they had shut up in the Committee of Public Safety, as in a defile, in order to murder them.' [1]

It is not difficult to imagine Robespierre explaining the finer points of the situation to Saint-Just when the latter returned to Paris in the early days of February, 1794. The *Indulgents*, some inspired by genuine humanity, some by foreign gold perhaps, were pleading for a relaxation of the Terror. In the Convention deputies who were troubled by the thought of the heads falling day after day echoed the appeal. Saint-Just grasped and dissected the situation with his usual stark logic. To him a weakening of the Terror meant a weakening of morale. It would be followed, almost certainly, by changes in the government. Only one argument could combat it: the war was not yet won; the final effort was wanting, the spring offensive on which Carnot was prepared to risk everything. To hesitate or fumble was to lose all; the Allies unless checked at the outset would march on Paris in May, and the Revolution would be extinguished in defeat and obloquy. These facts were so clear to Saint-Just that he felt they could not fail to appeal with equal force to all men of good principles. The Terror had to be maintained because the only alternative to it was military defeat and the destruction of all

[1] *Papiers inédits trouvés chez Robespierre, Saint-Just, Payan, etc., supprimés ou omis par Courtois* (3 vols., Paris, 1828), II, 36–37.

the Revolution had achieved. It may be Saint-Just accepted this rationalization sincerely, oblivious to the uglier, more fundamental fact that they had to guillotine others or be guillotined themselves.

On February 22, the Convention ordered its Committees of Public Safety and General Security to present a report on the thousands of political prisoners awaiting trial in the various houses of detention. Many of these victims, the *Indulgents* professed to believe, were innocent and deserved their liberty. Saint-Just, deputed to explain the policy of the Committees in the matter, decided to make his speech a justification of the Terror. His reply was delivered on February 26, and was one of the most effective discourses he ever read.

He began by minimizing the severity of the existing régime.

Citizens, by what illusion could one persuade himself that you are inhuman. Your Revolutionary Tribunal has condemned three hundred rascals to death in a year. Has not the Spanish Inquisition done worse than that, and great God, for what a cause! Have the English assizes butchered no one in that period? What of Bender, who roasts Belgian babies? What of the dungeons of Germany where people are entombed, do you ever hear of them? What of the kings of Europe, does any one prate to them of pity? Ah, do not allow yourselves to grow softhearted!...

To see the indulgence that some few advocate, you would think they must be the masters of our destinies and the high priests of liberty. Our history since the month of May last is a lesson on the terrible extremities to which indulgence leads. At that period Dumouriez had abandoned our conquests; patriots were being assassinated in Frankfort; Custine had surrendered Mayence, the Palatinate, and the banks of the Rhine; the Calvados was in revolt, the Vendée victorious; Lyons, Bordeaux, Marseilles and Toulon were in arms against the French People; Condé, Valenciennes and Le Quesnoy had capitulated; we were meeting with reverses in the Pyrenees and around Mont Blanc;

everyone was betraying you and it seemed as if men took charge of the government and the armies only to destroy them and prey upon the wreckage. The navy had been bribed, the arsenals and ships were in ashes; the currency was discredited, foreigners controlled our banks and our industries. But the greatest of all our misfortunes was then a certain fear of concentrating the authority necessary to save the State. The conspirators in the Party of the Right had blunted in advance, by an unsuspected stratagem, the weapons which you might use later to combat and punish them.... There are today some who would like once more to shatter these weapons.[1]

Saint-Just was not exaggerating the dangers which France had faced less than a year earlier. From these perils the iron rule of the Committee had rescued the nation, an achievement that outweighed many evils. But Saint-Just's discourse was more than a rational justification of the government policies, it was a finger-post on the road to the Utopia of the Robespierrists. 'Abolish beggary,' he commanded, 'it is a disgrace to a free state. The property of good citizens is sacred, but the goods of conspirators are there for the unfortunate. The poor are the powerful of the earth. They have the right to speak as masters to governments that neglect them.'[2] He concluded with a decree which confiscated the wealth of all recognized enemies of the Revolution and placed it at the disposal of the government. As a concession to the critics of the Terror, he proposed that the Committee of Public Safety should be authorized to liberate all prisoners who could give a satisfactory account of their activities from May, 1789.

This discourse of February 26 foreshadowed further repressive measures on the part of the Committee. Convinced that a vast plot existed to undermine the revolutionary government, the decemvirs decided to request the Convention for wider discretionary powers. Saint-

[1] O.C., II, 236–37.   [2] O.C., II, 238.

Just was again chosen as spokesman, and on March 13 read to the Convention his famous report *Sur les factions de l'étranger*. At the close of it the deputies voted, 'unanimously,' the records affirm, 'and in the midst of loud applause,' the draconic orders that provided a legal basis for the Great Terror.[1]

Yet Saint-Just had offered nothing in the form of genuine evidence to substantiate his story of a vast counter-revolutionary conspiracy financed with foreign gold. His discourse proved that the decemvirs were in a state of highly nervous apprehension, and that they saw every doubtful incident as a link in a chain of enemy activity that was fettering the Republic. To destroy a plot so monstrous the twin committees proposed to declare 'enemies of the fatherland' all those convicted of corrupting the citizens, of attempting to weaken or change the form of government, give aid to *émigrés*, or break open the prisons. Those who fled from justice were proclaimed *hors de loi*; every citizen was commanded to denounce such fugitives under penalty of death as their accomplice. This terrible decision exposed twenty-three fugitive Girondists to execution the moment they were discovered, and brought about the death of Masuyer and Condorcet within the month.[2]

The most terrible aspect of the new law was that it could be used not against enemies of France only, but against enemies of the Committee. Armed with the authority to crush their opponents, the decemvirs prepared to strike two swift blows, one to the Left and one to the Right. The fight with the factions had approached its *dénouement*.

[1] *Moniteur*, March 14, 1794.
[2] Claude Perroud, *La Proscription des Girondins*, pp. 178–81.

CHAPTER X
THE FIGHT WITH THE FACTIONS: THE DÉNOUEMENT

La Révolution est glacée; tous les principes sont affaiblis; il ne reste que des bonnets rouges portés par l'intrigue.

SAINT-JUST. [1]

By careful trimming, the decemvirs had managed to balance the *Indulgent* and *Enragé* factions with fair success until February, 1794. In the previous December the *Enragés* had been brought to heel by the arrest of Vincent and Ronsin. Happy at this discomfiture of their political foes, Desmoulins and Philippeaux then grew insolent, so that the Committee found it necessary to daunt the *Indulgents* by arresting Fabre d'Eglantine in January. But the balance between the factions was difficult to maintain, for the *Enragés* were not well organized and lost ground steadily. To strengthen them, the Committee of Public Safety released Vincent and Ronsin on February 4, on the thin pretense that no charge had been preferred against them. The decemvirs' policy was to divide and rule rather than to destroy.

The *Enragés* demonstrated promptly that they were too arrogant and too impetuous to play the decemvirs' game for them. Delirious at what they supposed to be their triumph, they plotted the supreme folly of an insurrection, and so precipitated their own destruction. For their attempted revolt was still-born; the Jacobins denounced it and the sections declined to respond. As a result the ringleaders were left defenseless before the wrath of the Committee, which had lost patience with them. Ronsin, Vincent, Hébert and a dozen of their cronies were arrested on the night of March 13–14.[2]

[1] O.C., II, 508.

[2] *Moniteur*, March 7, 1794; Buchez et Roux, *Histoire parlementaire*, XXXI, 331; Levasseur, *Mémoires*, III, 40-41.

The charges which the prisoners were called upon to answer before the Revolutionary Tribunal were coloured by the issues of the day and do little to clarify the facts. The Hébertists perished because they had opposed the centralized control of the Committee of Public Safety. Their extravagant parade of patriotism and their sacrilegious buffoonery had disgusted a majority of the *Conventionnels*; their attempts to regulate prices and to frighten profiteers increased the famine and alienated the populace. When Carnot made good his control of the armies their last chance for a successful *coup d'état* vanished. Their arrest was an anti-climax, the most significant feature of which was that it left the Committee of Public Safety and the faction of the *Indulgents* alone in the arena.

A good case can be made out, with the aid of a century of research, to prove that the conspiracy of the *Indulgents* never existed except in the fevered imagination of Robespierre and the icy phrases of Saint-Just. Certainly, to impartial posterity, the judicial murder of Danton appears the blackest item that can be urged against the Robespierrists. For his share in that tragedy Saint-Just has long since answered at the bar of history and been condemned. He read before the National Convention the denunciation which sent the Dantonists to the guillotine. From that it is impossible to absolve him; but it is possible by a reëxamination of the evidence to explain his motives and divide his responsibility.

In November, 1793, four deputies of the Convention were arrested on the charge of intriguing with foreign agents. They were Chabot, Bazire, Delauney (of Angers) and Julien (of Toulouse). Chabot, in his attempts to extricate himself, confessed that a vast plot existed, which aimed at the dissolution of the National Convention through organized calumny and systematic corruption. In January, Fabre d'Eglantine was denounced for his embezzlement of funds in connection with the French East

India Company, which convinced Robespierre that the 'Conspiracy of the Foreigner' was a reality, and that the *Indulgents* were involved. He communicated his fears to Saint-Just, who revealed them to the Convention in his gloomy and ominous report of March 13, 1794. This discourse, though filled with dark hints of prison conspiracies and plots to murder the Jacobins and leaders of the Convention, contained nothing whatever that could be designated as proof. The decemvirs were acting upon a suspicion because they dared not wait to see it confirmed.

From his cell in the Prison of the Luxembourg, Chabot wrote Saint-Just, affirming virgorously the reality of the conspiracy while denying his own connection with it.[1] At the same time, Danton drew suspicion upon himself by defending his friend Fabre. He urged the deputies to permit the prisoners to appear before the Convention, and denounced the attempt to involve Fabre and Chabot in one vast conspiracy as puerile. Billaud-Varennes did not hesitate to rebuke Danton publicly. 'Woe to the man who has sat at the side of Fabre and is still his dupe,' he proclaimed. Once again the prestige of the Committee enabled it to bear down all opposition, so that Danton's motion to bring Fabre before the Convention was lost.[2]

The 'Conspiracy of the Foreigner' was still an hypothesis in January, 1794, but evidence poured in to confirm it. The persistent attacks of the Opposition Party in the Convention convinced Robespierre that this faction was led by traitors. Most of the assaults wasted themselves against the Ministry of War, or Marine, or Foreign Affairs, but a single breach in the defenses thus adroitly interposed would have left the Committee of Public Safety dangerously vulnerable. The proof of this is to be seen in the promptness with which Barère or Billaud-Varennes or Robespierre would appear in the fray opportunely, like

[1] Bibliothèque de Nantes, Collection Labouchère, MSS. 675–156 and 675–157.
[2] *Moniteur*, January 13, 1794.

the gods from Olympus, whenever the battle threatened to turn against their satellites.

The ill-judged insurrection of the Hébertists was further proof to Robespierre that the 'Conspiracy' had wider ramifications than even he had suspected. 'The faction of the *Indulgents* which desires to save the criminals, and the faction of the foreigner [the *Enragés*] which makes a pretense of violence because anything else would betray it, but which turns its severity against the defenders of the people — all these factions meet at night to concert their activities. They pretend to fight each other to distract attention, then they connive to extinguish liberty between two crimes.' [1]

The *Indulgents* in the Convention and the *Enragés* at the Hôtel de Ville were regarded as being all bound up in the same conspiracy, an amazing conjecture, certainly, yet one that Saint-Just proclaimed on March 13 as if the facts were in his hands. The foreigner had forced his perfidious way into the strongholds of liberty, into the Commune of Paris which had saved the Revolution on July 14, 1789, on August 10, 1792, and on June 2, 1793; and into the National Convention itself. What hope was there for the armies fighting so valiantly on the frontiers when this hydra-headed faction flourished at Paris, vaunting its immunity? But the decemvirs had a revelation to make that was even more paralyzing. The long arm of the foreigner had reached into the Committee of Public Safety itself, and a member of that Committee was betraying its secrets to the Allied Powers!

His colleagues fixed upon Hérault-Séchelles as the traitor. He had been an object of suspicion to Saint-Just and Robespierre since December, 1793, because of the manner in which he conducted his diplomatic missions. For the moment they were content to exclude him from the deliberations of the Committee, while they sought for

[1] O.C., II, 266.

evidence that would connect him with the 'Conspiracy of the Foreigner.' Proof was still lacking in March, but Hérault himself provided grounds for his arrest. He was found to be concealing a refugee from justice, and this, under the new decrees of March 13, made him an accomplice. He was arrested March 15.

Hérault was probably innocent of wrongdoing, but Fate, which had made him a noble, a sybarite and a scoffer, had foredoomed him to Robespierre's dislike. Someone, certainly, was betraying the secrets of the Committee to the enemy. Throughout this period weekly reports found their way to London which described the developments in Paris from day to day, and even the deliberations of the Committee which met in the *Pavillon de Flore*. In occasional details these reports are correct enough to prove a definite leakage of information, probably through some subordinate close to the Committee. When accurate information was lacking, the spy padded his packet of news with ingenious guesses. It seems more than probable that the espionage system comprised several agents who gleaned facts and hints around Paris, transmitted them to a neutral country, and thus took all the risk. In Switzerland, or one of the Rhine cities, a master-spy prepared a synthetic report which was sold to the Allied governments.

In the absence of verifiable information, the spies sometimes fell back upon fabrication and forgery. Thus in the spring of 1794 a manuscript was circulated among the Allied diplomats which purported to contain a discourse delivered a few weeks previously by Saint-Just in the secrecy of the Committee of Public Safety. The writer aped Saint-Just's style so cleverly, and discussed with such intimate knowledge the inner workings of the French diplomatic service, that the forgery remained undetected until recent years. Saint-Just was represented as denouncing the vast sums of gold which the Republic had found it necessary to expend to maintain its influence in neutral

countries; the propaganda value of such disclosures naturally won for the report a warm welcome from the English
and Prussian governments, and translations of Saint-
Just's *Discours sur les relations avec les puissances neutres*
appeared promptly in Germany and England.[1]

Surrounded by spies and goaded by the tactics of the
Opposition, the decemvirs were driven to use terror as
their weapon where persuasion was beginning to fail. The
fiction of a responsible Executive Council could not be
maintained much longer, and they had decided to sup-
press it and erect twelve commissions of government under
the direction of the Committee of Public Safety. While
they waited an opportune moment in which to propose
the change to a critical Convention, the *Indulgents* opened
a new attack upon them. In this skirmish of March 18–22,
Danton took an active part, and this, coupled with the
fact that the Committee had gained confidence from its
victory over the Hébertists, helped to decide his fate.

The campaign opened by the Opposition in the session
of March 18 followed the usual formula. Danton, Delacroix and Bourdon (de l'Oise) first attacked the Minister
of War, then turned their criticism against the Committee
of General Security. At the following session they secured
the arrest of an agent working for the latter committee.
The lightning was striking too near home to please the
decemvirs; Couthon and Robespierre came forward to
compel the reversal of the decree, and as usual won their
point. But both were nervous and acrid in their rebukes,
and Danton's charge that the Committee denied freedom

[1] Saint-Just's authorship of the 'Discourse on the relations with the Neutral
Powers' was accepted by Charles Vellay in his edition of the *Œuvres complètes de
Saint-Just* (Paris, 1908), II, 333–50; and by Gaston Vidal in his more recent
brochure, *Saint-Just* (Paris, 1923), p. 164. For the evidences of its falsity con-
sult Albert Mathiez, 'Un faux rapport de Saint-Just,' *Annales révolutionnaires*,
VIII (1916), 599–611; and Geoffrey Bruun, 'Une traduction anglaise du faux
rapport de Saint-Just rédigé par d'Antraigues,' *Annales historiques de la Révolution française*, N.S., IV (1927), 275–77.

to the press by hushing up the eloquence of the Opposition leaders was too true to be altogether pleasant.[1]

On the evening of March 30 the members of the Committee of Public Safety and the Committee of General Security held a joint session. It was decided to arrest four deputies of the National Convention, Danton, Delacroix, Desmoulins and Philippeaux, and to accuse them of a conspiracy to obtain a change of government by corrupting and dissolving the Convention. The decree was signed by eight members of the Committee of Public Safety and ten from the Committee of General Security. Saint-Just was entrusted with the task of preparing an announcement and explanation of this measure, to be delivered to the Convention on the morrow. The arrests were to be effected before daylight.

One of the victims, Delacroix, managed to communicate the news of his arrest to his friend Legendre before the gates of the Luxembourg closed upon him. 'The moment has come when everything must be told,' he pleaded, 'and the Committees relieved of the tyrannical powers of which they make such monstrous use.'[2] When the Convention opened its session on March 31, Legendre tried to introduce a motion to bring the accused deputies into the hall so that they might have an opportunity to defend their innocence. But Robespierre, Barère and Saint-Just were present to deflect such a move, and Saint-Just had brought with him a report upon which he had expended his ultimate efforts.

The twenty-eight pages of the *Rapport sur la conjuration ourdie pour obtenir un changement de dynastie* are too carefully polished to permit the supposition that Saint-Just composed them *after* the Committee meeting of the

---

[1] The *Moniteur* mutilated Danton's speech of March 18 against the Minister of War beyond all coherence. The *Journal des débats et décrets*, No. 545, gives a fuller account.

[2] The letter is printed in the *Annales révolutionnaires*, XII (1920), 60–61.

previous night. Moreover, there is internal evidence to suggest that he prepared the oration in the belief that he would deliver it while Danton was present in the Convention, and much of it is addressed to the arch-conspirator personally. The thought of Cicero's oration against Catiline was in his mind, no doubt, and he had the supreme effrontery to dream himself capable of facing down Danton's volcanic fury. His colleagues on the Committees did not share his confidence it would seem, preferring to silence Danton in advance. In the absence of the accused, Saint-Just's successive evocations — 'Thou, Danton' — took on the appearance of a rhetorical device.

'Danton, you are answerable to an inevitable and inflexible justice. Let us look at your past conduct and we will prove that since the first day, allied with every conspiracy, you have been the enemy of the party of liberty; that you plotted with Mirabeau, with Dumouriez, with Hébert and with Hérault-Séchelles.' [1] For nearly thirty pages Saint-Just strung out his spectacular and damning accusations, until they were sufficient to have blasted the reputation of the Incorruptible himself. For Danton's conduct before September, 1792, he had to rely upon hearsay, for he had not been a witness, and Robespierre provided the gossip. He did more: he prepared for Saint-Just a handful of notes upon which to base the charges against the Dantonists, and to the outline of the report he added comments and emendations. The discourse owed its form and eloquence to Saint-Just, but the inspiration was Robespierre's.[2]

The pusillanimous Convention heard the report to the end and then voted the decree which committed to the

[1] O.C., II, 315–16.

[2] Albert Mathiez, 'Les notes de Robespierre contre les Dantonistes,' *Annales révolutionnaires*, X (1918), 433–68. The notes were first published in 1841, Chez France, Libraire-Editeur, Paris, under the title, *Projet rédigé par Robespierre du rapport fait à la Convention Nationale par Saint-Just, contre Fabre d'Eglantine, Danton, Philippeaux, Lacroix et Camille Desmoulins.*

Revolutionary Tribunal five of its members, Desmoulins, Hérault, Danton, Philippeaux and Delacroix. For some reason — it can scarcely have been for old friendship's sake — Saint-Just placed Camille's name at the head of the list, though Fabre d'Eglantine was considered the originator of the conspiracy and Danton was the most famous member. Five days later the Convention gave a further proof of its weakness by voting — 'with applause' the records affirm — a decree which denied the prisoners a longer trial, and authorized the Tribunal to send them back to prison and sentence them in their absence.

The Committee of Public Safety, by striking swiftly and firmly, had cowed the Convention. Two days after the arrest of the Dantonists, and before their execution, Carnot proposed the decree which revised the whole machinery of government. 'The six ministries and the Provisory Executive Council suppressed, and replaced by twelve Commissions attached to the Committee of Public Safety — there,' he summed up, 'is the system.'[1] The decree was to go into effect within three weeks, and all measures necessary to its fulfilment were entrusted to the Committee. France was to be governed by a decemvirate, but a decemvirate, as Barère pointed out, 'responsible at every moment, deriving all its authority from the National Convention, and reporting everything to it.'[2] Barère never showed to better advantage his talent for distorting facts and displaying them under the most favourable aspect.

[1] *Moniteur*, April 3, 1794. Session of April 1.
[2] *Ibid.*, April 1. Session of March 30.

CHAPTER XI

THE SYLLOGISTIC PARADISE

Dieu, protecteur de l'innocence et de la vérité, puisque tu m'as conduit parmi quelques pervers, c'était sans doute pour les démasquer!

SAINT-JUST.[1]

'IT IS not enough, citizens, to have destroyed the factions, it is necessary now to repair the evil that they have done to the country.'[2] With these words Saint-Just opened, on April 15, the last great drive of the Robespierrist group to establish the Utopia of their dreams. His speech was crowded with all the old formulas, the visions of a liberated world, the homage of a grateful posterity, the nobility of virtue and the dignity of devotion, but the phrases had begun to lose something of their edge and the bankruptcy of the ideologist program was apparent. For the only practical measure he could suggest that would unlock the millennium was a more ruthless application of the Terror.

In scanty moments of leisure, he had found time to draft a constitution for the Utopian society in which 'law did not make right but right made law.' As of old his conceptions were bookish and immature, and his indebtedness to authors ancient and modern made his chapters a patchwork of plagiarized passages. For all his precocity, Saint-Just at twenty-six was still an adolescent dreamer; but had Fate permitted his thoughts to ripen towards a maturer utterance he might have left literary monuments of some worth, for he had sincerity and perseverance. To the last he remained a poet at heart, stirred by inspirations that possessed a native vitality and were not devoid of grandeur. The gift of original expression he never perfected, but he belongs of right in the lesser ranks of that

[1] O.C., II, 494.   [2] O.C., II, 367.

Platonic brotherhood who have dreamed in every age of a 'city laid up in heaven.'

Once or twice, as he sketched the vague outlines of his *Institutions républicaines*, he permitted incidents from his youth to touch the austere design with a spot of personal colouring. The recollection of his mother's curbing hand was lively in his mind when he ordained that male children ought to be separated from their parents at five years of age and educated by the state. Pride in his eloquence inspired a suggestion for an annual prize in oratory, to be awarded for the best example of laconic prose; and his lack of humour allowed him to propose in all seriousness (he never jested) that invalided soldiers should wear a gold star sewn to their uniforms at the point of injury. But in fairness it should be remembered that the 'Republican Institutions' were the fruit of swift and stolen hours. The truly amazing thing about them is the frequency with which the intensity of his poetic conception coloured and transfigured the faulty and trivial details.

Saint-Just's hunger for dreams was the authentic nostalgia of the idealist. The fragments of his dream have a. nimbus of glory, and gleams from the Age of Gold invest the fields and farms of his Arcadian country. He saw the people assemble, grave elders and chanting children, for the annual festival of liberty. He saw the slow procession pause before the temple gates, there to offer incense to the Manes of those who first made them free and equal. At times the dream possessed him so completely it stole him from himself. 'The man, obliged to cut himself off from the world and from himself, casts his anchor in the future, and clasps to his heart a posterity innocent of our present vices.'[1]

The discourse of April 15 ended like the rest with a demand for more extensive powers, and the Convention voted the twin Committees all they asked. These decrees

[1] O.C., II, 494.

of April 15, because they were less dramatic than the Law of 22 Prairial, have been somewhat slighted by historians. They provided that all persons suspected of being enemies of the Revolution were to be tried by popular commissions in their native communities, and unless cleared of the charges against them, were to be despatched to the Tribunal at Paris. To clear the prisons, the two Committees appointed a few weeks later a special commission for the city of Paris, which was to hasten the judgment of captives already held. The decisions of all these courts were subject to the ratification of the Committees, but as they were always confirmed the responsibility for the sentences lay with the Popular Commissions.

It was a vicious system, the more so because no official could clearly envisage his own share of the responsibility. The judges of the popular tribunals assumed that their decisions merely referred cases to a higher court — the Committees — and the Committees endorsed the lists submitted to them on the supposition that the cases had already been judged and were to be carried to an appellate court, the Revolutionary Tribunal. When an accused came before this final seat of judgment, his guilt was presumed, and the percentage of acquittals steadily decreased.

Saint-Just's share in shaping the legislation upon which the Terror rested has already been suggested, but he had also a more direct responsibility. A number of denunciations had been accumulating in the files of the Committee of Public Safety from all parts of France, and in April, 1794, the decemvirs established a special bureau of police to deal with these. They placed in charge, on Saint-Just's recommendation most probably, a certain Augustine Lejeune, who later left an account of his services in a memoir of doubtful veracity.[1] Lejeune had known Saint-Just in earlier days, and remembered him as a gentle

[1] Alfred Bégis, 'Saint-Just et les bureaux de Police Générale,' *Annuaire: Société des amis des livres* (Paris, 1896), pp. 63–85.

youth whose modest ambition it was to live one day in the country, and who had desired only 'A wife and children, to fill my affections, study for my leisure hours, and something beyond my needs, that I might give it to my good neighbours if they were unfortunate.' But in Paris, Lejeune found a different Saint-Just, who had repudiated his dream of a country life 'in order to regenerate a people corrupted by centuries of barbarity and slavery.' It is evident Lejeune was no very profound student of character: the transformation in his young friend puzzled him severely.

The existence of this Bureau of General Police has been the principal argument of those interested to prove Robespierre and Saint-Just responsible for the Great Terror. Yet Lejeune admits in his memoir that they interfered little in the control of the Bureau, which, he maintained, although it examined a number of cases, sent none to the Tribunal. Robespierre, who supervised its working from April 29 to June 30, signed, according to his own statement, some thirty orders for the arrest of conspirators or the release of patriots, and his assertion has been substantiated by an examination of the records. After Robespierre retired at the end of June, Saint-Just took over this duty for less than four weeks, but the Bureau by this time was functioning adequately and he gave it but cursory attention.

At its worst, the Bureau of General Police was a very small wheel in the machinery of the Terror. Had Robespierre and Saint-Just retained sole charge of it, their colleagues on the two Committees would still have to answer for their share in creating the other commissions and tribunals. 'The mere name of the General Police,' Robespierre complained on July 26, 'has served as a pretext for laying on my head the responsibility for all the operations of the Committee of General Security, of all the constituted authorities, and of all my enemies.' [1]

[1] Charles Vellay, ed. *Discours de Robespierre* (Paris, 1908), p. 412.

Before Thermidor, Robespierre's enemies had begun to lay upon his head all the blame for the work of the guillotine, but after his overthrow even his colleagues lent themselves to the task of building up the legend. The Law of 22 Prairial in particular was denounced as his handiwork, and Barère and Billaud-Varennes did not hesitate to declare that the Committee as a whole was opposed to it. 'Is it not known to all,' they demanded audaciously, 'ever since the sessions of Fructidor 12 and 13, that the decree of 22 Prairial was drawn up secretly by Robespierre and Couthon, and that in defiance of all custom and all right it was never discussed nor submitted to the Committee of Public Safety?' [1]

Unfortunately for their defense, the contemporary records tell a different story. The Law of 22 Prairial was proposed to the National Convention by Couthon on June 10, 1794. The great number of cases referred to the Revolutionary Tribunal at Paris was proving more than that Court could despatch, and Couthon therefore urged that the Tribunal should be divided into four sections, each composed of three judges and nine jurors. Only enemies of the people were to come before the reconstructed court, but this class was broadened to include all those accused of attempts to reëstablish royalty, to dissolve the Convention, overthrow the government or corrupt the morals of the people. Couthon concluded by reading twenty-two articles embodying the changes, naming the new judges and jurors, and recapitulating specifically the crimes of *lèse nation*, the penalty for which was to be death.[2]

'If this law is adopted without adjournment,' a deputy cried as Couthon left the tribune, 'I will blow out my

[1] 'Réponse de Barère, Billaud-Varennes, Collot d'Herbois et Vadier aux implications de Laurent Lecointre,' *La Révolution française*, XXXIV (1898), 168.

[2] *Moniteur*, June 12, 1794.

brains.'[1] The Convention was shaken and irresolute, and several urged a postponement of the discussion. But Barère, who was later to urge that the project had been drawn up secretly without the knowledge of the Committee, rose to defend it. 'When a law is proposed,' he declared, 'wholly favourable to patriots and fraught with prompt punishment for conspirators, the legislators can be nothing if not unanimous in their vote upon it.'[2] Robespierre, following Barère, presented the deputies with a choice between two dangers. 'The National Convention,' he said, 'stands in the shadow of assassination, for the moment when liberty is about to triumph most gloriously is the moment when the enemies of the country conspire with the greatest audacity.... It is not natural to find a divergence of opinion among men equally imbued with love of the public welfare. It is not natural that a sort of coalition should raise its head against a government wholly devoting itself to the safety of the nation. Citizens, your enemies are trying to divide you, to work upon your fears.' At the cries of 'No, no!' he changed his attitude a little, and turned to discuss, in more conciliatory and explanatory tones, the attempts which had been made a few days earlier to assassinate members of the Committee. 'We have made ourselves a special mark for assassination by pursuing the public assassins. We are ready to die, so that the Convention and the country may be saved. We will even brave the calumnies that some wish to attach to the measures demanded by public safety, for the severity of these measures holds no threat save for conspirators, for enemies of liberty and of humanity.'[3]

The passage of the Law of 22 Prairial was the last and in some respects the greatest of Robespierre's triumphs. Article by article it was discussed, and then voted without alteration by an obedient Assembly. But the following

[1] *Moniteur*, June 12, 1794.   [2] *Ibid.*   [3] *Ibid.*

day, when no members of the Committee were present, a selfish fear for their own safety drove the deputies to modify one section. On the motion of that persistent recalcitrant, Bourdon (de l'Oise), it was settled that no deputy should be liable to arrest without a preliminary decree of the Convention. The Committee promptly rallied to meet this reverse, and on June 12, Couthon, Robespierre, Barère and Billaud-Varennes attacked the amendment and secured its revocation. The debate was tense and bitter, the deputies knew they were fighting for an immunity the loss of which would leave them individually helpless, and the members of the Committee knew that the smallest defeat, if unredressed, might start a landslide that would sweep them out of office. The struggle between the Convention and its Committee of Public Safety had taken on the nature of a duel; the popularity of the decemvirs was waning, and the only weapon left to them was intimidation.

Saint-Just had no part in these acrimonious debates, for he was away once more on a mission to the armies. The spring campaign had opened, and the republican generals, in obedience to Carnot's strategy, were preparing to concentrate on the northern sector for the valiant drive which saved the Revolution and started the French armies on their career of conquest. Saint-Just, by an ironic twist of fate, was to participate personally in the great victory of Fleurus, the repercussion from which, when it reached Paris, was to shatter the Committee of Public Safety and throw the Robespierrists to the guillotine.

CHAPTER XII

FLEURUS

La journée de Fleurus a contribué à ouvrir la Belgique.

SAINT-JUST, July 27, 1794.[1]

AT THE end of April, Saint-Just and Le Bas were again ordered to the Army of the North. The hour had struck for the supreme effort, and the preparations were complete for the spring offensive which was to prove a turning-point in the history of the Revolution. 'A mediocre triumph,' Carnot warned the generals, 'would be our destruction.'[2] His plan of campaign was to withdraw all available men from the Rhine and concentrate them against the Allied forces, 145,000 strong, which held the Belgian frontier. He relied upon the Polish situation to hold the Prussians inactive in Alsace, and this surmise, though justified, was an example of that republican audacity which baffled the commanders of an older school. So thin was the cordon left to defend the line from Longwy to Kaiserslautern and Wissembourg, that 'a single enemy corps of four battalions could have broken it anywhere.'[3] Disaster in this form threatened late in May to nullify the whole plan of campaign, but Carnot declined to be turned from his purpose and the danger passed.

Notwithstanding the high spirits pervading the French forces, and the preparations for an early offensive, the first success of the spring went to the Allies. On April 19, Pichegru wrote the Committee that the enemy had crossed the Sambre and was attacking Landrecies. Before the end of the month the town surrendered, and this drive in

[1] O.C., II, 483.   [2] Aulard, *Recueil des actes*, XII, 42.

[3] Gouvion Saint-Cyr, *Mémoires sur les campagnes des armées de Rhine* (4 vols., Paris, 1829), II, 12.

the centre destroyed for the time the alignment of the republican armies. Jourdan, marching to reinforce the Army of the North, was forced to recoil upon Longwy. Pichegru hesitated in a disconcerted fashion and suggested counter-attacks on the enemy's wings. But Carnot urged patience; he had a double revenge in preparation.

To draw the forces and attention of the Allies to the far northern sector by a feint attack in Maritime Flanders, while launching his real drive in the angle between the Sambre and Meuse, was Carnot's project; but several ill-concerted manœuvres were still to threaten it before success could be achieved. As usual the army had to be purged of conspirators and keyed to the requisite degree of enthusiasm. The loss of Landrecies was promptly traced by Saint-Just to treachery and disorganization among the troops defending the Cambrai sector. As the loss of the latter city would have shattered the republican centre beyond repair, Carnot was alarmed for its security. 'The place is very strong,' he wrote Saint-Just and Le Bas May 2. 'We do not fear for its reduction save through treason, and we rely upon your presence to frustrate that.'[1] The two envoys redoubled their efforts. From their head-quarters at Réunion-sur-Oise they poured forth a stream of orders, and they erected a military tribunal to deal out punishment to aristocrats and enemy agents.

But the reëstablishment of an army's morale was too small a task for Saint-Just's energies; he wished also to direct its operations. While announcing the fall of Landrecies, he had urged an attack upon Maritime Flanders as the best counter-stroke, to be accompanied by a drive on Valenciennes. Carnot rejected the suggestions tactfully, and Saint-Just immediately commenced, in conjunction with Pichegru, to devise another plan.[2] The Committee had proposed a concentration at Beaumont, in order to force the passage of the Sambre. Apparently Saint-Just

[1] *Correspondance générale de Carnot*, IV, 341.　　[2] O.C., II, 411.

planned instead to attempt the crossing at Thuin, and march thence to Charleroi. But to Carnot such a passage appeared too costly, if not actually impracticable, and he insisted peremptorily upon his own strategy.

Meanwhile from the North came the cheering news that the Austrian attempt to cut Souham's detachment off from Lille had been defeated in soldierly fashion at Turcoing on May 18. Saint-Just felt that his chance to make a brilliant move on the Sambre was slipping away. After several days of indeterminate struggle he was able to write the Committee on May 22 that the river had been crossed. At once he saw himself directing a drive upon Mons and Brussels, and he revealed the plan to Jourdan, who, pushing valiantly north with the Army of the Moselle, had progressed as far as Dinant. But his elation was premature. The Allied forces counter-attacked, and the French were thrown back from the Sambre with a loss of twelve hundred men.[1]

On May 31 the Committee recalled Saint-Just to Paris. There is no evidence that his colleagues were dissatisfied with his efforts; the real reason for his recall was a new threat from the factions, which were intriguing more actively than ever. It is probable that Saint-Just had an opportunity to discuss at this time the provisions of the Law of 22 Prairial which Couthon was to propose to the Convention a week later. But he could not wait to defend the measure with his eloquence. The army claimed him, and before the 10th of June he was back on the Sambre, with his powers extended to include the supervision of all operations from the Rhine to the North Sea.[2]

During his absence the prospect on the Sambre had brightened. Up from the South in the early days of June

[1] Wallon, *Les représentants du peuple en mission*, IV, 240.

[2] The letter recalling Saint-Just to Paris is printed in Buchez et Roux, *Histoire parlementaire*, XXXV, 404; the order sending him back to the army, in Aulard, *Recueil des actes*, XIV, 171.

came the Army of the Moselle under the impetuous Jourdan. His instructions were to attack Namur; but Austrian resistance drew him across the Meuse, and Carnot then changed his orders and sent him against Charleroi.[1] Under his command the dispirited Army of the Ardennes was joined with that of the Moselle, and the two became the immortal Army of the Sambre and Meuse. The passage of the Sambre was attempted with new vigour. By June 12 the river had been crossed at several points; by June 17 Charleroi was invested. Events were hastening to a climax.

The activities of Saint-Just are hidden in the stirring movements of these June days. He laboured energetically as usual to improve the morale of the soldiers, and he attempted to supervise the siege operations about Charleroi. But he knew little of military engineering and the manœuvres had grown too rapid and too complex for him to follow. Such at least is the impression conveyed by his letters to the Committee.[2] Nor was he kept fully informed of the Committee's plans, a fact which, when he later discovered it, seemed to him to be fraught with a sinister significance and formed the basis of his attack upon Carnot in his speech of the Ninth of Thermidor.

The circumstances which caused this wound to Saint-Just's vanity were the result of an oversight on the part of Carnot. With his usual fertility of expedients, Carnot had developed a plan for a sudden descent upon Holland, which he outlined in a despatch to Pichegru and the representatives Richard and Choudieu on June 17.[3] But the expedition required the deletion of at least 18,000 men from Jourdan's command, which the latter could ill spare at a moment when Charleroi was almost within his grasp. Realizing this, Carnot postponed the project before Jourdan or the representatives with him had heard of it at all, for it had appeared unnecessary to distract them from

[1] *Correspondance générale de Carnot*, IV, 373 and 382.
[2] O.C., II, 429–37.   [3] *Correspondance générale de Carnot*, IV, 433.

their main purpose. Only on his return to Paris after Fleurus did Saint-Just discover that Carnot had been on the point of weakening Jourdan's army at a moment when such an action might have nullified all the sacrifices of the campaign.

For Jourdan, in the last week of June, 1794, was forcing the decisive action of the summer. The bombardment of Charleroi, commenced the 23d, proceeded with fury.[1] The garrison was outnumbered and discouraged, for Coburg still held his major divisions in the North where the brilliant tactics of Moreau and Souham culminated on June 17 in the capture of Ypres. Too late Coburg turned south to face Carnot's major offensive on the Sambre. When he approached Charleroi on the 26th he found the republican lines completely surrounding the city, and he gave battle unaware that the garrison had capitulated the day before.

The battle of Fleurus lasted from dawn to dusk and ended in a signal victory for the French. The Austrian army was repulsed and scattered, and the defeat so lowered the morale of the Allied forces that they fell back rapidly, leaving Belgium open to the Republicans. For the first time in over two years France was free from the danger of invasion and the excuse for the Terror was at an end. In July, therefore, the centre of interest shifts once more to Paris, where the repercussion of the victory was to produce the political reversal of the Ninth of Thermidor. Saint-Just, with the faculty already noted of divining each new centre of strife, forsook the Army of the North two days after the battle and rode rapidly to Paris, arriving late in the night of June 29–30.

His colleagues at the Committee of Public Safety were still in session. Barère recounts in his memoirs how they welcomed Saint-Just, demanding information about the

[1] Bibliothèque municipale de Rouen, MSS., *Fonds Girardin*, Autographes Nos. 802–04.

battle and urging him to present a report on it to the Convention in person. But he refused doggedly. 'He seemed moody,' Barère declared, 'and wrapped in thought.'[1] Perhaps his sullenness was born of fatigue and nervous exhaustion; or it may be that he sensed a new spirit in the heated air of that Green Room of the *Pavillon de Flore*, which bore out certain hints he had received from Robespierre and made him distrustful. Constraint and suspicion had fallen upon the decemvirs in the interval while he was away. They watched each other warily, held together still by the principle of cabinet responsibility, but separated into groups with the lines of cleavage widening. Saint-Just had to adapt himself to the new currents, decide where his loyalty lay, and plot a course that would carry him through the period of transition that was approaching. But he had only four weeks in which to catch up with events; the crisis which already darkened the horizon was to task the diplomatic genius of Barère, and Saint-Just had neither Barère's experience nor his adroitness. When the storm broke he managed to ride out the first day of it, cool and clear-headed. The second swept him under.

[1] Barère, *Mémoires*, II, 18.

CHAPTER XIII
THUNDER ON THE LEFT

Les malheurs de la patrie ont repandu sur tout l'empire une teinte sombre et religieuse.
SAINT-JUST.[1]

THE idealistic fervour of the Revolution was clearly on the wane in the spring and early summer of 1794, and in the National Convention Robespierre's prestige, which was based, as the deputy Baudot shrewdly observed, on a revolutionary fantasy, was waning with it.[2] This relaxation of tension, accompanied by a growing spirit of discord, alarmed the decemvirs, who fell back upon artificial stimulants in an effort to revive the faltering morale. Such was the festival of the Supreme Being; and the importance given to several attempts at assassination, from which members of the Committee escaped during these months, prove that they felt it necessary to advertise their services and court new popularity.

The most bitterly hated figure on the Committee was Robespierre who bore the blame for the maintenance of the Terror. A growing list of intriguers were working for his overthrow, and several of his colleagues on the Committee would gladly have seen him resign. But the necessity of presenting a united front kept the decemvirs from betraying the secret rivalries of the Committee, for they knew their enemies in the Convention would be swift to profit by them. The impeachment of Robespierre would have opened a breach in the Committee's defenses which would have invited further attacks, and ended with the complete reorganization of the executive power.

For this reason, the divisions within the *Pavillon de*

[1] O.C., II, 537.

[2] Marc-Antoine Baudot, *Notes historiques sur la Convention nationale*, p. 4.

Flore were hidden, and several attempts made to heal them. Robespierre withdrew from Committee meetings at the end of June, his vanity hurt by the conviction that he and his friends Couthon and Saint-Just were being shouldered out of affairs there; but he forbore to criticize his colleagues and made no move to resign. The reorganization of the government, proposed by Carnot at the beginning of April, had been carried out, and twelve commissions erected to centralize the administration in the hands of the decemvirs. But Robespierre had little genius for administration and saw the new machinery as something which menaced his supremacy. Couthon was sick and bedridden much of the time, and Saint-Just, when he returned from his mission to the armies, found himself a minister without portfolio. Far from dominating the Committee, the triumvirs, by the opening of July, 1794, were an ineffective minority.

Perhaps it was Barère's plan to reduce Robespierre's influence until he and his friends could be eliminated without destroying the Committee. Efforts were made to separate the discontented trio by sending Couthon on mission to the Midi, a proposal that bore no fruit. Saint-Just's return to the Army of the North was earnestly besought by his fellow representatives there, but he refused to leave Paris. Prieur (de la Marne), who might have supported Robespierre, was away on mission; Jeanbon Saint-André left for Toulon July 6; and a day later the departure of Couthon for the Midi was again decreed. But Couthon, like Saint-Just, preferred to remain in Paris; and Robespierre the Younger, whose presence was awaited by the Army of Italy, did the same. The party of Robespierre, already in a minority in the Committee, would not permit itself to be further weakened.

Yet Robespierre took no active measures to strengthen his position. Apparently he placed all his reliance upon the speech which he was preparing for the National Convention. At the Jacobin Club he continued to hint darkly of a conspiracy to divide the patriots and destroy the foremost friends of liberty. July 11, he and Couthon attacked Dubois-Crancé, and persuaded the Club to expel him. Fouché was invited to attend and answer the charges against him, but he refused on the plea that his case was in the hands of the Committee. Robespierre complained that such a reply constituted an attempt to set the Jacobins against the Convention, and Fouché was expelled from the Club also.[1]

It would appear that even at the Jacobins, his last stronghold, the ardour of Robespierre's following was cooling somewhat. His brother Augustin complained bitterly at the indifference that was evinced while patriots were being persecuted; and Couthon declared melodramatically that he would share the daggers that were in wait for the Incorruptible. On July 24, Couthon grew more alarmed. All the artillery was being moved out of Paris, a sinister step for which there appeared to be no adequate motive. The rumour was gaining currency that a fatal breach had developed in the Convention and within the Committees. Still true to the principle of cabinet responsibility, Couthon affirmed his confidence in the latter, but he admitted that the Convention held half-a-dozen wretches who deserved to be crushed.

Until Robespierre's speech of Thermidor 8 (July 26, 1794), no member of the Committee of Public Safety had publicly reproached his colleagues. As late as July 22, Barère warned the Convention against the reports that were being circulated to the effect that misunderstandings and divisions reigned in the Committees. Such lies, he maintained, were the work of enemies who sought to destroy the Revolutionary Government — 'that bridge of bronze by which the French People have passed from a corrupt monarchy to a regenerated Republic.'[2] To set at

---

[1] Aulard, *Société des Jacobins*, VI, 218–21.   [2] *Moniteur*, July 24, 1794.

rest all uncertainty regarding the Committees, he announced that they had held a joint session that morning, and had decided to submit to the Convention within the week a comprehensive report on the affairs of the nation and the government. Similarly, Couthon, in his speech at the Jacobin Club the following night, was careful to exempt his colleagues from his insistent but ambiguous accusations. Despite private differences between Robespierre and Billaud-Varennes, or between Saint-Just and Carnot, the principle of united responsibility still determined all public utterances of the decemvirs. 'We would have felt we were betraying our mandate if we had shattered the unity of the government,' Prieur (de la Côte d'Or) confessed later. 'With us, sentiments of political necessity dominated all others.'[1] It was this careful preservation of an apparent harmony that made the Ninth of Thermidor appear like a sudden thunderstorm gathering out of a clear sky. But a truer metaphor was suggested by Robespierre on Thermidor 8 when he declared that they were all walking on a volcano. Echoes of its rumbling had reached as far as Brussels and London.

'I am sending you, my dear colleagues,' the representative Gillet wrote the members of the Committee of Public Safety on July 11, 'three numbers of the *Mercure Universel* printed at Brussels. You will learn in Number 361, with a surprise doubtless equal to mine, that Bourdon (de l'Oise) and Tallien are regarded by our ferocious foes as the champions of a faction which may, in their opinion, succeed in overturning the Committee.'[2] Gillet's news can have held little surprise for Robespierre who had accused Bourdon a month earlier of conspiring to make himself the head of the Opposition Party. The members of the Committee were also in possession of letters written by Fouché

[1] L. H. Carnot, *Mémoires sur Carnot* (2 vols., Paris, 1861), I, 521.

[2] Aulard, *Recueil des actes*, XV, 89. The letter is quoted in part by Albert Mathiez in his study *Autour de Robespierre*, p. 169.

to his sister, informing her of the progress of his plots. In the middle of July he wrote of his refusal to plead his case before the Jacobin Club — 'because there Robespierre is the master. That Society,' he added, 'has become his tribunal. In a little you will learn the issue of these developments which will turn, I trust, to the profit of the Republic.' [1]

By July 21, Fouché was able to write with more assurance. 'A few days yet,' he predicted, 'and truth and justice will achieve a striking triumph.' And July 23 he added, 'Inside of two or three days the wretches will be revealed and the integrity of honest men triumph. Today, perhaps, the traitors will be unmasked.' [2] With his talent for intrigue Fouché was a dangerous opponent for any government. 'I did not scruple,' he confessed in his memoirs, 'in contending for my head, nor in long and secret deliberations with such of my colleagues as were threatened with my own fate. I merely said to them — among others to Legendre, Tallien, Dubois-Crancé, Danou and Chenier: you are on the list, you are on the list as well as myself; I am positive of that.' [3] Fouché's Memoirs are a tissue of deceit, but for once he seems to be telling the truth.

That a cabal had been formed with the object of breaking the power of the Committees was known to royalist spies as early as June 16. 'More than fifteen members of the Mountain must be guillotined,' affirmed a secret despatch of that date, 'or the Committee of Public Safety will be overthrown.' Two weeks later the spy wrote again: 'Lecointre de Versailles and fifteen others are at the head of the discontented faction, not openly, but breathing in secret all their hatred against Robespierre and their indignation against the Committee of Public Safety.' [4]

[1] Aulard, *Recueil des actes*, XV, 345.   [2] *Ibid.*, 453.
[3] Joseph Fouché, *Memoirs* (2 vols. London, 1825), I, 18.
[4] Quoted by Albert Mathiez, *La conspiration de l'étranger* (Paris, 1918), p. 215.

Intriguers as clever as Fouché, Tallien and Bourdon (de l'Oise) were certain to seize upon the rumours of a rift in the Committee and draw new hope from them. If his colleagues were prepared to turn against Robespierre a sudden stroke from the Convention would find him defenseless.

The decemvirs, sensing the insidious pressure to which the Committee was being exposed by those who wished to break it apart, made a last valiant effort to heal their discords. On July 22, Saint-Just was entrusted by his colleagues from the two Committees with the task of preparing a report on the best means of repressing enemy agents and silencing calumnies against the government. The choice of Saint-Just for this responsibility indicates that a temporary reconciliation had been effected between the factions in the Committee of Public Safety. Billaud-Varennes attempted a friendly overture to Robespierre who had forsaken his seclusion to attend. 'We are your friends,' he urged, 'we have always marched in accord.' But his hypocrisy disgusted Saint-Just, who reminded him that the day previous he had been calling Robespierre 'Pisistratus'; and in the end the meeting broke up without the conclusion of a real truce.[1]

Balked in their attempts to split the Committee, the conspirators on the Mountain threw out friendly suggestions to the deputies of the Plain, urging an alliance strong enough to overturn the Committee altogether, in the event that Robespierre's colleagues refused to sacrifice him. Three times they returned to the charge before they finally persuaded Durand de Maillane, Boissy d'Anglas and Palasne-Champeaux to promise their support in an attack upon the Incorruptible. The members of the Plain, unaccustomed since the fall of the Gironde to any show of initiative, could be relied upon to follow the example of these three leaders, and a vote that won the support of the

[1] O.C., II, 487.

Plain would have weight enough to counteract Robespierre's prestige.

The delicate negotiations were still incomplete when Robespierre precipitated a crisis by his speech of Thermidor 8. The issue was joined and the battle opened with the intriguers still desperately uncertain how far their allies would aid them. In the outcome their understanding with certain members of the Committee saved them, for it paralyzed the Committee. The decemvirs spoke in contradictory terms; the Convention yielded to confusion; and the insurgent deputies seized the situation and forced through their proscriptions. The men of the Plain acquiesced as they had been taught to do. Yet so delicate was the balance, so dramatic the setting, and so charged with fate for the actors, that the events of Thermidor 8–9 marched forward like the scenes of a well-constructed play. 'The vicissitudes through which we passed,' Billaud-Varennes decided afterwards, 'would make a good subject for a tragedy. I will write that tragedy.' [1] But he never did.

'Robespierre, who had not appeared in the Assembly for a considerable time, mounts to the tribune....' So runs the opening sentence in the official accounts of the session of Thermidor 8. Numerous descriptions have made it easy to picture him as he faced the rising semicircle of benches, a small man of slight build who wore a sky-blue satin coat with well-starched ruffles and a neatly powdered wig. As usual he stood stiffly with his head held back, and he read with slow deliberation, pausing between the sentences. The Convention listened in a profound silence to the discourse which he himself named, with a premonitory conviction, his last will and testament.

'I have not come,' he hastened to assure his audience at the outset, 'to formulate those ridiculous threats which have been maliciously spread abroad; I wish only, if it be

[1] L. H. Carnot, *Mémoires sur Carnot*, I, 535.

possible, to extinguish the torches of discord in the pure light of truth.'[1] He laboured to dissolve the calumnies which had darkened his reputation and to shift the blame for the Terror to other shoulders. There was a conspiracy organized to destroy the friends of liberty; he knew the leaders of the conspiracy, he maintained, and that he was to be the foremost victim. It has been said too often that the greatest mistake committed by Robespierre in his speech of Thermidor 8 was his failure to name any of the men at whom his denunciations were levelled. This criticism is only partly correct. He denounced Amar and Jagot of the Committee of General Security, and declared that they were leagued with members of the Committee of Public Safety in a plot to spread dissension and calumny. Then, careless whom he antagonized, he attacked the economic policies of Cambon, of the Committee of Finance. The remedy for the prevailing injustice and corruption he summed up in a final sentence. 'To punish the traitors, renew the bureaux of the Committee of General Security, purge this Committee and subordinate it to the Committee of Public Safety, purify the Committee of Public Safety itself, and establish the unity of the government under the supreme authority of the National Convention.'[2]

The ring of sincerity in Robespierre's words swayed the Assembly despite its prejudices. 'He had,' one deputy recorded, 'an air of such simplicity and fairness. He appeared to be so convinced of the soundness of his doctrine, that I have sometimes felt that he was perhaps more fanatical than ambitious, and that he aspired to govern France only because he believed in all sincerity that he alone could save her.'[3]

The motion was proposed amid loud applause that the discourse should be printed, an honour accorded by the

[1] Charles Vellay, *Discours et Rapports de Robespierre*, p. 381.   [2] *Ibid.*, 427.
[3] Arnaud Meillan, *Mémoires*, p. 6.

Convention to all important reports. Bourdon (de l'Oise) opposed the motion; Barère supported it; and Couthon persuaded the deputies to vote that the speech should not merely be printed, but that copies should be distributed throughout the departments. Robespierre's star appeared to be still in the ascendant; to his enemies it seemed as if his one discourse had undone all their efforts. Vadier, of the Committee of General Security, who had been ridiculing Robespierre for weeks, now hastened to make his apologies; but Cambon, of the Committee of Finance, was more courageous. 'I demand to speak,' he cried, leaping to the tribune. 'Before being dishonoured, I will speak to France.' After defending his financial policies which Robespierre had impugned, he dared to put the charge against the latter into words. 'It is time that the whole truth was told. A single man is paralyzing the will of the National Convention; that man is the same who has just read the discourse: it is Robespierre.' [1] The statement was a declaration of war and Cambon knew it. That night, on the copy of the *Moniteur* which he mailed to his father at Montpellier he scribbled the significant words: 'By tomorrow either Robespierre or I will be dead.' [2]

Inspired by the example of Cambon other deputies found the courage to assert themselves. One after another Billaud-Varennes, Panis, Bentabole and Charlier rose to criticize the discourse; and Bréard finally suggested that to distribute it throughout France as Couthon had proposed would lend to its charges an official endorsement which the Convention did not intend them to bear. A second vote was taken and the decree for distribution reversed. Contented with this technical victory the deputies closed the session of the Convention at five o'clock. The first act of the drama was at an end.

[1] *Moniteur*, July 29, 1794.
[2] F. Boneral, *Cambon et la Révolution française* (Paris, 1905), p. 343.

CHAPTER XIV
THE TARPEIAN ROCK

Le cours des choses a voulu que cette tribune aux harangues fût peut-être la Roche Tarpéienne pour celui qui viendrait vous dire que des membres du gouvernement ont quitté la route de la sagesse.

SAINT-JUST, July 27, 1794.[1]

FOR the developments during the night of Thermidor 8–9 (July 26–27, 1794) the sources are fragmentary and largely undependable, but it is possible to reconstruct an outline of the events. The populace of Paris was in a restless mood, partly as a result of the unusual heat, the temperature for days having stood abnormally high even in the early morning.[2] Robespierre, whose energies were unimpaired, hastened in the evening to the Jacobin Club, where he re-read the discourse which the Convention had heard that afternoon. The enthusiastic reception accorded it by the Society restored his faith in his oratory. Billaud-Varennes and Collot d'Herbois, who also attended the meeting, attempted to reply to his veiled charges, but they were hooted down and left the Club pursued by threats. Without loss of time they sought the *Pavillon de Flore*.

There they found Carnot, Barère and Prieur (de la Côte d'Or), discussing the situation in low voices. Saint-Just, who was also present, had been engaged since eight o'clock drafting a speech which he planned to read to the Convention the following morning. His colleagues, knowing the close understanding which existed between him and Robespierre, were apprehensive regarding the contents of his discourse, but they hesitated to question him. At one o'clock, however, the quiet of the committee room was broken by the agitated entrance of Collot and Billaud,

[1] O.C., II, 477.

[2] *Journal de Physique*, I, 429, Paris, an II (1794).

still shaken by the turn events had taken at the Jacobin Club, and Saint-Just glanced up from his writing.

'What's new at the Jacobins', Collot?' he called across the room in a casual voice. The calm indifference of the query turned Collot's fear to sudden anger. 'He saw how deeply I was agitated,' he admitted afterwards, 'and he was marble.' Striding swiftly forward he seized Saint-Just by the arm, determined to know the worst, and peered hurriedly at the closely written pages that littered the table.

'You are drawing up our act of accusation!' Saint-Just attempted to shuffle together the sheets of the report, but Collot persisted. 'You can't fool us! That is our indictment!' There was a moment's pause, and then Saint-Just rose coolly to his feet.

'Well, yes, you are not altogether wrong, Collot,' he admitted. 'I am drawing up your accusation.' Then, turning upon Carnot with calm arrogance, he added, 'You are not forgotten either, and you will find that I have treated you in masterly fashion.' [1]

This spiteful thrust brought Saint-Just's colleagues crowding about him with a demand to see the report. As it was to be presented in the name of the Committee, this was no more than their right, and Saint-Just, regretting his revelations, was driven to temporize. He explained that the discourse did not propose a decree of accusation against any member of the Committee, though it criticized some of them. It was, moreover, still unfinished, and too illegible to read; but he promised that he would have his secretary reduce it to order, and that he would submit it to the Committee at ten the following morning for approval. With this promise his companions contented

[1] L. H. Carnot, *Mémoires sur Carnot*, pp. 532–34, quotes a memoir of Prieur (de la Côte d'Or) describing this dispute. Prieur's account, too dramatic in its form to escape suspicion, is clearly substantiated by Collot's statement in the Convention given the following day. *Moniteur*, July 30, 1794. Session of July 27.

themselves, and between four and five Saint-Just gathered up his papers and left to seek a few hours' sleep.

For the enemies of Robespierre the situation was too uncertain to permit repose. Before ten in the morning the members of both Committees assembled unofficially and discussed the perplexities in which they found themselves, but they failed to come to any decision.[1] The indefatigable Fouché was also present and doubtless appreciated the situation.[2] It was evident that the Committees were still determined to remain neutral; if Robespierre was to be overthrown the attack would have to come from the threatened deputies of the Convention. The web of intrigue so carefully spun during the previous weeks was to be subjected to a sudden test; for if Robespierre and Saint-Just were permitted to speak they might reëstablish their domination over the Convention and the conspirators would be lost.

The session of the Ninth of Thermidor opened in the Convention about ten o'clock with the transaction of some unimportant business. In the *Pavillon de Flore* the assembled Committees continued to wait for Saint-Just and his report. At eleven he had not appeared; it was approaching noon when a messenger brought a note from him. 'Your injustice,' he reproached his colleagues, 'has sealed my heart. I am going to open it to the Convention.'[3] As they realized the trick by which they had been kept waiting two hours, the members of the Committees rose in indignation. 'Let us go,' one of them is reported to have said, 'and unmask these villains, or else present our heads to the Convention.'[4] The words have an apocryphal

[1] 'Réponse de Barère, Billaud-Varennes, etc.,' *La Révolution française*, XXXIV (1898), p. 160.

[2] Speech of Collot d'Herbois to the Convention July 27, reported in the *Moniteur*, July 30, 1794.

[3] 'Réponse de Barère, Billaud-Varennes, etc.,' *La Révolution française*, XXXIV, 160.

[4] 'Réponse de Barère, etc.,' p. 160; Barère, *Mémoires*, II, 219; *Mémoires sur Carnot*, I, 553.

ring but the indignation may have been genuine enough. As Robespierre set out for the Convention on the morning of July 27, his landlord Duplay urged him to take some precautions against the plots of his enemies, but the warning was disregarded. Apparently his reception at the Jacobin Club the previous evening had restored the Incorruptible's confidence in himself and his principles. 'The majority of the Convention is pure,' he assured Duplay. 'It will support me. I have nothing to fear.'[1]

Actually, a majority of the deputies had already been persuaded to support his enemies. The Committees, it was evident, would not declare themselves, but it is possible they gave some sort of assurance that they would not defend Robespierre if he were attacked. 'In the morning of the 9th, the Committee saw several members of the Convention,' Robert Lindet wrote cryptically in his brief memoir on the events of day.[2] It is significant also that Tallien knew, when he interrupted Saint-Just at the tribune, that the latter's speech had not been approved by the Committee, a fact he could have learned only in the *Pavillon de Flore*.[3]

The understanding which the conspirators had developed with the leaders of the Plain was of an equally nebulous variety. 'On the 9th of Thermidor,' the deputy Thibaudeau recorded, 'the great majority of the Convention were entirely unprepared for what happened. It burst upon them like a clap of thunder.'[4] But Durand de Maillane has confessed his foreknowledge, and had promised his assistance. To the conspirators the tacit sympathy of the Plain was invaluable. Durand was

[1] Baudot, *Notes historiques*, p. 242; Buchez et Roux, *Histoire parlementaire*, XXXIV, 3.

[2] Montier, *Robert Lindet*, p. 249.

[3] Session of July 27, reported in the *Moniteur*, July 29, 1794.

[4] Antoine-Claire, comte de Thibaudeau, *Mémoires sur la Convention et le Directoire*, ed. by Berville et Barrière (2 vols., Paris, 1824), I, 82.

walking in one of the galleries of the Convention on the morning of the 9th when Bourdon (de l'Oise) approached him and gripped his hand. 'Ah, the men of the Right, what splendid fellows they are!' he babbled; and a moment later Tallien and Rovère came up with the same desire to seal the understanding which they had fostered. But at that juncture they caught sight of a movement in the Assembly. 'There is Saint-Just at the tribune!' Tallien exclaimed. 'It is time to make an end of this.' And he rushed away.[1]

Like Robespierre, Saint-Just was overconfident. On the previous occasions on which he had addressed the Convention it had never failed to hear him and grant the decrees he proposed. But his victories had been won by the force of an arrogant mind that beat down opposition, and the memory of them filled his audience with a latent hostility. If he felt this resentment around him he made no effort to exorcise it; he had never learned how to disarm or cajole an audience. Straight to the tribune he marched, carrying his head, as Desmoulins had written, like the holy sacrament; and having mounted it he turned to survey the Convention coolly with the air of faint contempt which had become habitual. He was dressed with care and correctness in a buff coat, white vest, and dove-coloured breeches.[2]

'I belong,' he commenced, 'to no faction. I will make war upon all of them.... Circumstances have conspired to make this tribune a Tarpeian Rock, as it may well prove, for the orator who comes to warn you that some members of the government have forsaken the course of wisdom.'[3] He could proceed no further, for Tallien had arrived upon

[1] Pierre-Toussaint Durand de Maillane, *Histoire de la Convention nationale* (Paris, 1825), p. 198 f.

[2] Henri Wallon, *Histoire du Tribunal révolutionnaire de Paris* (6 vols., Paris, 1881), V, appendix V, pp. 440–44.

[3] O.C., II, 447.

the scene. His voice cut across the weaker accents of Saint-Just. 'I demand the floor on a motion of order!' he shouted. 'The speaker has commenced by declaring that he is of no party. I say the same thing. I belong only to myself and to Liberty. That is why I am here to proclaim the truth. No honest citizen can refrain from tears at the prospect of public affairs. Everywhere there is division.... I demand that the veil be entirely torn away.'[1]

The Assembly was in confusion. Unfortunately all the official records of the session are incomplete and undependable; but it becomes clear from a careful collation of the reports that the opposition to Robespierre was neither so spontaneous nor so unanimous as the Thermidorians afterwards suggested. When Tallien concluded his brief speech, he was succeeded by Billaud-Varennes, who denounced the agitation at the Jacobin Club, warned the Convention that an insurrection was being plotted, and attacked Robespierre mildly. The latter attempted to reply, but the tribune was accorded to Tallien again. The conspirators had determined that no Robespierrist was to be permitted to speak, and to enforce their will they depended upon Collot d'Herbois who for that fortnight was President of the Convention. Tallien's second speech was filled with vague allusions to the danger threatening the Republic. He demanded that the Convention vote itself in permanent session until the conspiracy was unmasked, and this decree was adopted.[2]

As Tallien left the rostrum he was again replaced by Billaud-Varennes. Barère, ever the compromiser, sought to counsel Billaud as he moved forward to speak. 'Do not attack anyone except Robespierre; let Couthon and Saint-Just alone,' the deputy Espert heard him whisper.[3] Billaud thereupon denounced Hanriot, General of the

---

[1] *Moniteur*, July 29, 1794.   [2] *Ibid.*

[3] E. B. Courtois, *Rapport... sur les évènemens du 9 thermidor* (Paris, an IV [1796]), p. 39.

Army of Paris, and demanded his arrest, which was voted by an Assembly still uncertain whither all the charges were tending. A cry was raised that Barère must take the stand and explain the situation in the name of the Committees. His speech is a proof that to this astute politician Robespierre's overthrow seemed still improbable. He defended the Committees, urged that in a time of uncertainty it was most necessary to have confidence in the constituted authorities, and promised a refutation of the criticism which Robespierre had levelled the previous day against his colleagues. He concluded by proposing that the Convention should issue a proclamation to the people of Paris, denouncing the designs of a few military leaders against the national authority, and urging the populace to remain tranquil. His proposals were adopted with cheers.[1]

Barère's attempt to calm and reassure the Assembly had a considerable effect; but the insurgent deputies, having opened the attack, had no intention of permitting the session to close with a tacit victory for the government. Vadier, of the Committee of General Security, rose to defend himself against Robespierre's insinuations of the previous day, and moved the Convention to laughter with his references to the affair of Catherine Théot. But Tallien, who was the stage-manager of this tragedy, had no desire to see it degenerate into a farce. 'I demand the floor,' he interrupted, 'in order to lead the discussion back to the real issue.' 'I will lead it back!' cried Robespierre, starting towards the tribune. For the third time the President ruled in favour of Tallien.[2]

The accounts of the remainder of the session are so contradictory, and so obviously worked over, that it is impossible to reconstruct any satisfactory picture of it. Robespierre's arrest was proposed; his brother demanded to share it, and the decree was voted — unanimously, the

[1] *Moniteur*, July 29, 1794.
[2] *Ibid.*

records affirm.[1] There must have been some hesitation, however, for a few minutes later the arrest of Augustin Robespierre was put to the vote a second time. Then Le Bas, the friend of Robespierre and Saint-Just, made his voice heard. 'I refuse to share the infamy of this decree,' he declared. 'I demand to be arrested also.'[2] There seems to have been further hesitation. Differences of opinion showed themselves. But Fréron, Billaud, Louchet and Elie Lacoste reiterated the vague accusations that had been levelled at the Robespierrist group, and the arrest of the two Robespierres, Saint-Just, Couthon and Le Bas was announced as carried. Another pause ensued. Robespierre still strove to speak, but his words were lost in the insistent clamour of the President's bell. Then the guards of the Convention were ordered to lead out the prisoners. They hesitated to obey, until the five deputies surrendered themselves and were conducted from the hall. It was four o'clock.[3]

'Nothing,' records Courtois, describing this session, 'was more beautiful, more majestic, than the calm of the Convention. After having struck down Robespierre and his accomplices, it turned peaceably to its business.... The Roman senate had not greater dignity....'[4] Barère's recollection of the close of the session was somewhat different. 'The Assembly,' he wrote, 'stunned, or perhaps terrified, by its temerity and its decrees, separated at five o'clock.'[5]

The comic relief in this Roman tragedy is provided by the admirer of Robespierre, and commander of the armed forces of Paris, the sans-culotte general Hanriot. The day had commenced inauspiciously for this ex-lackey, and it was to close more inauspiciously still. He had scarcely

---

[1] *Moniteur*, July 29, 1794; *Journal des débats et décrets*, No. 676.
[2] Buchez et Roux, *Histoire parlementaire*, XXXIV, 35.
[3] *Journal des débats et décrets*, No. 677.
[4] E. B. Courtois, *op. cit.*, p. 46. [5] Barère, *Mémoires*, II, 224-25.

returned from his breakfast when he was accosted by three agents from the Committee of General Security who presented an order for his arrest. Rising in fury, the general ordered the men immediately executed, according to their own account, and when his staff protested he mounted his horse and galloped off, waving his sabre.[1] Since early morning he had held the armed forces of the sections in readiness; after two o'clock he began to assemble them at the Hôtel de Ville.[2] There he addressed them with drunken eloquence, but it is significant that he did not reassure them as to the purpose for which they had been called out. Shortly after four, learning of Robespierre's arrest, Hanriot set a squadron of cavalry in motion and led it at a gallop towards the Convention.[3]

On his arrival at the Tuileries, Hanriot attempted to enter the offices of the Committee of General Security, but was stopped by the gendarmes on guard. Thereupon the general commanded his men to dismount and help him force his way in.[4] Some half-dozen obeyed; but as soon as they had entered the building, the whole party was seized and disarmed by the guards of the Convention. The credit for the arrest was later claimed by an agent of the Committee of General Security named D'Ossonville. 'I gave an order to the gendarmes to disarm them,' he boasted, 'and to tie them up with their own belts, like so many bales of tobacco.'[5]

Hanriot's attempt to rescue the five arrested deputies

[1] 'Rapport au Comité de Sûreté générale par le citoyen Héron, chargé d'arrestation de Hanriot.' Quoted by G. Lenôtre, *Vieilles maisons, vieux papiers* (4 vols., Paris, 1900–1910), III, 327–28.

[2] L. Lecointre, *Robespierre peint par lui-même* (Paris, 1794), p. 5; *Papiers inédits trouvés chez Robespierre*, III, 305.

[3] *Papiers inédits trouvés chez Robespierre*, III, 308. Deposition of Ulrick, aide-de-camp of Hanriot.

[4] C. A. Méda, *Précis historique des évènemens qui se sont passés dans la soirée du neuf thermidor* (Paris, 1825), p. 22.

[5] 'Fragments des mémoires de d'Ossonville,' *Revue de la Révolution*, III (1884), p. 11 (Documents).

thus ended in swift and signal failure. Without further resistance the Committee of General Security despatched Robespierre under guard to the prison of the Luxembourg. Saint-Just was sent to that of Ecossais; Couthon to La Bourbe; Le Bas to La Force; and Robespierre the Younger to Saint-Lazare. Hanriot was imprisoned with several of his men in one of the rooms of the Committee of General Security. By seven o'clock the third act of the revolutionary drama was at an end.

CHAPTER XV

THE APPEAL TO ARMS

Les circonstances ne sont difficiles que pour ceux qui reculent devant le tombeau.
SAINT-JUST.[1]

THE action of the Convention in decreeing the arrest of the Robespierrists should have set at rest all doubts on the part of the remaining members of the Committee of Public Safety as to which side it would be expedient to favour. The fact that they continued to hesitate, at a moment when decisive action alone could have enabled them to recapture the Committee's waning prestige, must be attributed to the confusion which had paralyzed them since the preceding day. The strain, the uncertainty, and the physical weariness resulting from lack of sleep, may have unfitted some of the members for resolute action; but their hesitation may have had another cause also. Though arrested, Robespierre was not yet condemned. Marat had faced the Revolutionary Tribunal and emerged triumphant. It is possible that for an hour or two after the close of the session a compromiser like Barère may have entertained the idea of arbitrating between the followers of Robespierre and the insurgents in the Convention, so winning for the Committee a controlling voice in the dispute. But this plan, if he did indeed entertain it, was rendered impracticable by the rapid march of events.

Lecointre de Versailles was later to declare that the conduct of the remaining members of the Committee of Public Safety, after the removal of the triumvirs, revealed grave negligence if not actual treachery towards the interests of the Convention. They did nothing, he charged, either to secure the persons of the arrested deputies, or to frustrate the rebellion at the Hôtel de Ville of which they

[1] O.C., II, 494.

had been repeatedly warned.[1] In reply to this attack, Barère, Billaud-Varennes, and their colleagues proved that after the Convention closed its session at five o'clock on Thermidor 9, the members of the Committee of Public Safety and the Committee of General Security met at a joint conference to devise such measures as the situation appeared to demand. They ordered the arrest of Hanriot, alive or dead; forbade the ringing of the tocsin and the closing of the barriers, and ordered the Sections to submit an hourly report on the condition of Paris. They also instructed the military forces from four Sections to assemble before the Convention for its defense.[2]

These decrees, if they had been taken by the members of the two Committees on their own initiative, would constitute the best evidence of their decision and energy. But in reality the Committees, which had apparently held a permanent session from five o'clock on, permitted the situation to ripen unchecked, so that the Convention, hastily reassembled at seven, found itself faced by a popular insurrection the extent of which no one could for the moment ascertain. While the deputies heard with growing alarm the reports of insubordinate acts committed at the Hôtel de Ville, the gravity of the outbreak was brought home to them in dramatic fashion. At eight the Committees, still in session, were warned that the cannoneers of the Commune were approaching, and the assembled members fled to the Convention for protection. 'Citizens,' announced Collot d'Herbois, 'the time has come for us to die at our posts. The soldiers — the rebels — have invested the Committee of General Security and taken possession of it.'[3]

---

[1] 'Réponse de Barère, Billaud-Varennes, etc.,' *La Révolution française*, XXXIV (1898), 161.

[2] 'Réponse de Barère, etc.,' pp. 162 and 164; *Recueil des actes du Comité de salut public*, XV, 457, 460–61.

[3] *Moniteur*, July 29, 1794.

The panic-stricken manner in which the members of the Committees sought safety in the Assembly indicates how much of their arrogant authority had fallen from them. Voulland, of the Committee of General Security, proposed that the deputy Barras should be appointed to command the loyal forces of the Convention, and Barras agreed after some hesitation.[1] He left the Tuileries, and finding that the soldiers from the Commune had withdrawn, he prepared to rally what loyal troops he could assemble around the Convention, and to clarify public opinion by a show of discipline and decision. Shortly before midnight he returned to assure the Convention that it was defended by faithful Republicans, and that Paris would support the side of liberty. By midnight, therefore, it would seem that the tide of public opinion was setting in favour of the National Convention.

'The Committees,' Barras recorded, 'on finding the scene of the battle transferred from the Tuileries to the Place de Grève, recovered from their fright, and, as a consequence, at once resumed their insolent tone and taste for cruelty.'[2] It was probably at this time that they issued the greater portion of those decrees upon which they later based their claims of having foiled Robespierre's attempted revolution. But despite their able apologetics, Barère and Billaud-Varennes failed to make the rôle of the Committees on Thermidor 9 appear an effective one. It is not even clear that the members ever resumed their interrupted session at all, and the credit for defeating the insurrection at the Hôtel de Ville rested with the deputies in the Convention who had first attacked Robespierre.

There is some justification for the pride later expressed by the Thermidorians in their defiance of the Commune at a time when its forces were on the point of victory. The

[1] *Moniteur, loc. cit.*; Paul-François-Jean-Nicolas Barras, *Memoirs* (4 vols., New York, 1895), I, 221.

[2] Barras, *op. cit.*, I, 226.

news that Hanriot and Robespierre had been set at liberty drew from the deputies a decree setting them *hors la loi*. Though the cannoneers of the Commune were expected at any moment to bombard or invade the Tuileries, the Convention retained its dignity; and when the danger began to pass, and Barras brought word that loyal troops were rallying to defend them, the fear of the deputies turned to ferocity. Fréron promised that the Hôtel de Ville should be reduced to powder; Tallien urged that the soldiers should march against it at once, so that the heads of the conspirators might fall before dawn.[1] Had the enthusiasm and organization at the Commune been equally effective, nothing could have saved Paris from an armed conflict; but by midnight the forces assembled at the Place de Grève had begun to melt away, and Sections which had at first promised aid were reverting to a position of watchful neutrality.

It is a part of the Thermidorian legend that a popular insurrection had been planned for Thermidor 10, an insurrection which was to sweep Robespierre into power at the head of a triumphant Commune. The suddenness and success of the popular outburst which flamed up at the news of Robespierre's arrest lends verisimilitude to the story; but it is by no means evident that an armed revolt was prearranged: rather, it was precipitated. The deposition of Michel Bochard, *concierge* at the *Maison commune*, is interesting in this connection. 'The municipal body,' he swore, 'held a session on the 9th from one-thirty in the afternoon.... I heard nothing which had any relation to the rebellion that broke out that night during the session of the General Council of the Commune. Nothing wrong was done to my knowledge until towards evening.'[2] If this witness is to be trusted, it follows that the group in control at the Hôtel de Ville risked no illegal act

[1] *Moniteur, loc. cit.*
[2] Courtois, *Les évènemens du 9 thermidor*, pp. 200–01.

until it received the news of Robespierre's overthrow and Hanriot's arrest. On the receipt of this information, the Council General convened in special session about five-thirty, and from that hour there can be no doubt of its revolutionary intentions.[1]

The ostensible excuse for the activity which centred about the Hôtel de Ville on Thermidor 9 was the preparation of a civic fête. Two days earlier the General Council had requested permission from the Committee of Public Safety to convoke the assemblies of the Sections in order to discuss the project. [2] As Robespierre's name had been inseparably linked with the inauguration of the national fêtes and the Cult of the Supreme Being, the occasion was certain to awaken some popular demonstrations in his favour, which would lend him a moral support in his contest with the opposition faction in the Convention. The proposed activity of the General Council alarmed the Committees, but they hesitated to interfere on the ground of suspicion alone, lest a show of authority should provoke the insurrection which they feared. The Convention was less hesitant. At the session of Thermidor 9, it decreed the arrest of Hanriot, and the rigour of this measure was justified almost at once by the latter's invasion of the *Pavillon Marsan*, the first specific act of rebellion which had been committed.

At the Hôtel de Ville the decree against the five Robespierrists, and the report of Hanriot's capture by the gendarmes of the Convention, crystallized the sentiments of the group there. Confident that it controlled the armed forces of the city, the General Council ordered all the barriers to be closed, thus shutting Paris off from outside interference. The tocsin was rung, and the citizens urged to rally to the support of their magistrates. In defiance of the decrees of the Convention, Hanriot was declared

[1] Wallon, *Histoire du Tribunal révolutionnaire de Paris*, V, 229.
[2] *Papiers inédits trouvés chez Robespierre, etc.*, III, 292.

to be under the protection of the people, and messengers carrying the orders of the Convention were arrested. This activity of the General Council was shared by the Police Commissioners, who sent out instructions to all the prisons of Paris that no one was to be admitted or released except at their direct order.[1]

The effect of these actions of the revolutionary Commune was to disrupt completely the arrangements of the Convention. Robespierre, despatched under guard to the Luxembourg, was refused by the gaoler in charge, and taken to the offices of the Administrators of the Police, where, by eight o'clock, he was among friends, though he still insisted on remaining technically a prisoner. His brother Augustin, refused entrance at Saint-Lazare, was accepted at La Force, but was rescued almost immediately, and conducted by two police agents to the Hôtel de Ville. Saint-Just and Le Bas were released later. Couthon did not leave La Bourbe until after midnight.[2]

The liberation of Hanriot and his staff was achieved with even greater promptness and decision. Coffinhal, a judge of the Revolutionary Tribunal, was deputed to lead a detachment of two hundred cannoneers to rescue their general, and marching to the Tuileries between eight and nine o'clock, he forced an entrance into the Committee of General Security and unbound Hanriot. A few moments thereafter the general was once more on horseback, assuring his soldiers, with magnificent mendacity, that he had been paying the Committees a friendly visit, and had left them entirely satisfied with his conduct.[3]

The fortunes of the Commune were at high tide. With two hundred men at his command, Hanriot could have

[1] Buchez et Roux, *op. cit.*, XXXIV, 46–48; Courtois, *Les évènemens du 9 thermidor*, 101–02, 114–15.

[2] Courtois, *op. cit.*, pp. 112–14, 191–94, and 198.

[3] Courtois, *op. cit.*, Report of Dulac, p. 209; deposition of Viton, pp. 186–88; C. A. Méda, *op. cit.*, p. 28.

cleared the Convention and arrested the leading opponents of Robespierre against whom the Council General was issuing decrees of arrest.[1] But Hanriot let the opportunity escape him. It has been suggested that his spirits were somewhat dashed by his misadventures, and that he had no orders in any case to proceed to extremes. A third explanation, not to be ignored, is that his men were not clearly enlightened about the issue, and might have refused to obey him if he had ordered them to march into the National Convention itself. He drew off his forces, therefore, and before ten o'clock had galloped back to the Hôtel de Ville.

There he and Coffinhal were received with cheers. The General Council had accepted the responsibility of an armed revolt and had appointed a Committee of Execution. Having thus committed themselves past withdrawal, the members of the Council and their supporters were anxious to implicate the Robespierrists also in their project. But the latter, who perceived clearly the distinction between a moral demonstration and a military revolt, hesitated to join them. Augustin Robespierre, who arrived at the Hôtel de Ville about nine-thirty, declared that the Convention as a whole was sacred; the attack was to be directed only against the faction which had caused the arrest of his brother. Robespierre himself, who was still technically a prisoner at the *Mairie*, refused to break his arrest until the Council sent a deputation, accompanied by soldiers, to overpersuade him. Some time between ten and eleven o'clock he entered the Hôtel de Ville and joined the deliberations of the Committee of Execution.

In the same hour that it won the moral support of Robespierre's presence, the insurrectionary committee suffered a reverse of fortune. The decree of the National Convention setting the rebels *hors la loi* was proclaimed

[1] Wallon, *op. cit.*, V, 230.

throughout the city, and Barras began to win over the wavering Sections to the side of established authority. In a warfare of opinions, prestige is everything. The decree of the Convention, read aloud with due pomp on the street corners, to the light of flaming torches, convinced the restless section of the populace that neutrality might prove the wisest course. Among the troops gathered before the Hôtel de Ville, and already growing weary, the news deepened the sense of uneasiness which the irrational conduct of Hanriot had fostered. With their enthusiasm ebbing, the men turned about of their own accord and started back to their Sections. Hanriot, learning too late of their defection, rushed out of the Hôtel de Ville at one o'clock, sabre in hand and without a hat, and found the Place de Grève deserted.[1]

In the meantime the reluctant Barras, appointed to command the forces of the Convention, had drawn a scarf and a braided hat from the quartermaster's stores, and was preparing to play the soldier.[2] Having by midnight collected a force of loyal troops, he advanced cautiously towards the Hôtel de Ville. Léonard Bourdon, able at last to express his hatred of Robespierre in an active manner, collected a second contingent in the Gravilliers Section, and marched towards the same destination apparently by the rue Martin and the quai Pelletier. Meeting a company of retreating cannoneers on the way, he learned from them how matters stood at the Commune, persuaded them to join him, and a little before two o'clock deployed his column on the Place de Grève.[3] A deserter had betrayed to him the password for entering the Hôtel

[1] Courtois, *op. cit.*, Report of Dulac, p. 211.

[2] G. Lenôtre, *Les 9 et 10 thermidor, soixante-dix-sept facsimiles d'estampes et documents originaux réunis*, Plate 58.

[3] Barras, *Memoirs*, I, 225; C. A. Méda, *op. cit.*, pp. 30–32; Courtois, *op. cit.*, pp. 201, 204; *Papiers inédits trouvés chez Robespierre, etc.*, III, 308; *Moniteur*, August 4, 1794, report made by a delegation from the Section of Gravilliers on the events of Thermidor 9.

de Ville, and his men gained an entrance in silence and without opposition.

Unaware of these developments, the Committee of Execution, in the Assembly Room of the Commune, was organizing the insurrection and despatching vigorous decrees. All five of the proscribed deputies had collected there, Couthon arriving last about one in the morning. Saint-Just, who had been held with the others at the Committee of General Security until seven, and then despatched to the prison known as the Ecossais, was apparently released from it about ten and made his way directly to the Hôtel de Ville. With each succeeding hour the insurrection appeared to gather momentum, and by midnight the Committee of Execution was prepared to take those radical steps which, six hours earlier, would have overthrown the Convention. One order provided for the arrest of leading members of the Committees of General Security and Public Safety; others despatched representatives of the Commune to organize the Sections, and to maintain patrols on the streets. When Couthon arrived he joined Robespierre in drawing up an appeal to the armies. That the Convention might gather a force together and attack before daylight was a factor which they appear to have omitted entirely from their calculations.[1]

Shortly before two o'clock the activities of the Committee were interrupted by the return of Hanriot, crying that all his troops had deserted him and the forces of the Convention were approaching. This final ineptitude of the drunken general moved Coffinhal to uncontrollable anger. 'You fool, you have ruined everything!' he swore; and seizing Hanriot by the shoulders, he hurled him from the window. At the same time, the forces of Barras and Léonard Bourdon, which had occupied the lower halls of

[1] Buchez and Roux, *Histoire parlementaire*, XXXIII, 356; Courtois, *Les événemens du 9 thermidor*, Report of Dulac, p. 210.

the building, raised a cry of *Vive la Convention!*[1] Panic swept the group in the Assembly Room. Robespierre and the other deputies fled to the adjoining secretariat, where, realizing that escape was impossible, and that capture meant certain execution, three of them chose suicide. The loyal and resolute Le Bas shot himself. Robespierre, it seems probable, attempted to imitate him, but succeeded only in shattering his jaw with the pistol bullet. His brother Augustin climbed through a window, possibly with the thought of escape, but finding no means of reaching the ground, he hurled himself down with apparent deliberation, and was picked up seriously injured. The cripple Couthon was injured also, either by the soldiers who seized him, or in an attempt at escape. Saint-Just alone came through those moments of fear and turmoil without a wound. Barras found him ministering to Robespierre, and when the soldiers took him into custody he submitted indifferently and in silence.[2]

[1] Courtois, *op. cit.*, Deposition of Dumesnil, p. 184; *Moniteur*, August 1, 1794, speech of Barère in the Convention; Buchez and Roux, XXXIV, 59; *Moniteur*, August 4, 1794, Report of the Section of Gravilliers on the events of Thermidor 9.

[2] Courtois, *op. cit.*, pp. 203–05; *Papiers inédits trouvés chez Robespierre, etc.*, p. 72; *Moniteur*, July 30, 1794; Barras, *Memoirs*, I, 225–28.

CHAPTER XVI

FINALE

Je méprise la poussière qui me compose et qui vous parle; on pourra la persécuter et faire mourir cette poussière! mais je défie qu'on m'arrache cette vie indépendante que je me suis donnée dans les siècles et dans les cieux....

SAINT-JUST.[1]

THE remainder of the story is little more than an epilogue. When Saint-Just, having been marched through the streets along with Payan, the National Agent, and Dumas, President of the Revolutionary Tribunal, arrived at the *Pavillon de Flore*, he found Robespierre had been transported there already. The Incorruptible was stretched motionless upon a table in the audience room of the Committee of Public Safety; his head was resting upon a carton of army bread, and one arm was crooked over his shattered face. The rooms were filled by a throng of curious people, but the prisoners saw none of their colleagues there, for at the news of Robespierre's capture Barère and the others had sought their beds.

It was about five in the morning. Seated with his two companions in a window embrasure Saint-Just glanced about the room which had grown familiar to him in the course of a year. A few steps away, in a neighbouring alcove, was the desk at which he had sat twenty-four hours earlier preparing the discourse which Tallien had interrupted — a discourse surprisingly moderate in its conclusions. Had it been delivered, it would, in Aulard's judicious opinion, have averted the crisis, for Saint-Just was prepared to urge a dispersion of the autocratic powers which the exigencies of the war had concentrated in too few hands.[2] But the bridge was burned now; he was a

[1] O.C., II, 494.

[2] F. A. Aulard, *Les orateurs de la Législative et de la Convention* (2 vols., Paris, 1885–86), II, 472.

rebel captured in open insurrection against the national authority, and his strong sense of realism can have left him in no doubt as to the irretrievability of that circumstance. He appeared crushed, one witness noted; not outwardly, for his habiliments were in order and he preserved his usual air of composure, but broken in spirit. His eyes were bloodshot, as if with weeping, but it may have been the effect of two nights without sleep.

One of the prisoners asked for a drink of water, and while it was being brought Saint-Just's gaze fixed itself upon the *Declaration of the Rights of Man*, which, with the Constitution of 1793, was framed upon the wall. The instinct to justify himself fought with his depression for a moment. 'There, after all, is my work,' he muttered as if to himself. A glass of water was handed to him and after drinking a few sips he passed it back with a brief *merci*.[1] A few moments later he was despatched to the *Conciergerie*, the penultimate stop for those on the road to the *Place de la Révolution*. Inside its portals, one of the first figures he encountered was that of Lazare Hoche, with whom he had coöperated in the reconquest of the Wissembourg Lines the previous December. If the general felt any resentment against Saint-Just as a member of the Committee which had ordered his arrest, he forgot it at this moment and extended a friendly handclasp to a companion in misfortune.[2]

Robespierre, his wound washed and dressed, was likewise transported to the *Conciergerie* later in the morning. There, speech being impossible to him, he made signs that he wished to write something, but pen and paper were refused him.[3] His desire, it may well be, was to proclaim his innocence. When Augustin Robespierre, painfully

[1] 'Faits recueillés aux derniers instans de Robespierre et de sa faction,' Wallon, *op. cit.*, V, appendix V, pp. 440–44.
[2] Cuneo d'Ornano, *Hoche, sa vie et correspondance* (2 vols., Paris, 1892), II, 68.
[3] Wallon, *op. cit.*, V, 249.

injured from his fall, was interrogated by his captors, he protested that, like his brother, he had never ceased to serve the Convention loyally, and that those who carried him off from his prison had done him an evil service.[1] Couthon expressed a similar conviction. He swore that he had stubbornly refused to leave his prison because he had been sent there by a decree of the Convention, that he had endeavoured to respect that decree, and that he wished those who called him a conspirator could read his soul.[2] These men had been faced by a difficult dilemma and events had swept them into a position which no legal subtlety could justify. Fouché, in his judgment of the man he had laboured to overthrow, a judgment which he later found it expedient to modify, paid a tribute to Robespierre's helplessness. 'He had,' Fouché declared at the time, 'neither plan nor design: far from disposing of futurity he was drawn along with it, and did but obey an impulse he could neither oppose nor govern.'[3]

The victors were merciless in their triumph. Already the Thermidorian legend was in the process of manufacture. 'It is imperative,' Thuriot told the Convention on the morning of July 28, 'that the soil of the Republic should be purged of a monster who was on the point of proclaiming himself king.'[4] At the Duplay home, police agents were gathering up Robespierre's papers in a search for evidence of his sinister designs against the Republic; and at No. 3, rue Caumartin (then rue Thiroux), in the *Section des Piques*, where Saint-Just had furnished a comfortable suite of rooms for himself, other agents were sealing up his papers and impounding his possessions. This confiscated property was later sold, and the list has

[1] Courtois, *op. cit.*, pp. 204–05.

[2] 'Les derniers instants de Couthon,' *La Révolution française*, XVIII (1877), pp. 464–65.

[3] Fouché, *Memoirs*, I, 22.

[4] Germain Bapst, 'Inventaire des bibliothèques de quatre condamnés,' *La Révolution française*, XXI (1880), pp. 532–36.

a melancholy interest. Among Saint-Just's books the discourses of Demosthenes and Cicero bore witness to the classical inspiration of his oratory; his interest in mathematics was reflected by the presence of several books on that science; and Tasso's *Gerusalemme Liberata* suggested that he never outgrew his early affection for the poets.[1] Among his personal effects, an ivory flute hints at an accomplishment otherwise overlooked; and a field glass and sword recall his military activities.[2]

The triumphant Thermidorians persuaded the Convention to sweep aside all legal technicalities, and to vote that simple identification was the only process necessary for sending to execution prisoners who were already outside the law. Yet even with Barras at the Revolutionary Tribunal to urge expedition, it was late in the afternoon before the process was complete and the twenty-two condemned men started on the slow journey mounted in four carts. The guillotine had been moved for the occasion from the *Barrière-du-Trône-Renversé* to the *Place de la Révolution*: Robespierre was to be guillotined at the same spot as Louis XVI. Saint-Just, who had a place in the first cart, which carried also Robespierre and the mayor Lescot-Fleuriot, appeared calm and resolute.[3] The procession, which had started about six, took an hour and a half to arrive at its destination.

A large crowd had gathered to await the event in the ancient *Place Louis Quinze*, and the guillotine was set up to face the Tuileries. Couthon was executed first; his deformed body proved difficult to adjust on the plank and it required fifteen minutes to fasten him down. Augustin Robespierre was the second chosen. Saint-Just fol-

---

[1] Germain Bapst, 'Inventaire des bibliothèques de quatre condamnés,' *La Révolution française*, XXI (1880), pp. 532–36.

[2] G. Vauthier, 'La Succession de Saint-Just,' *Annales révolutionnaires*, XV (1923), pp. 513–14.

[3] Edmond Biré, *Journal d'un bourgeois de Paris pendant la terreur*, V, 398.

lowed him, calm, a little pale, but without weakness. He cast a glance of scorn over the heads of the crowd, and surrendered himself to the executioner.[1] The nineteen others were guillotined in the gathering twilight, while the crowd cheered, Robespierre and Lescot-Fleuriot being reserved until the end.

Thermidor marked the dissolution of the revolutionary fantasy and the end of the Reign of Virtue, but the Robespierrists were spared the ultimate bitterness of surviving the ruin of their syllogistic paradise. The spiritual nadir to which revolutionary idealism sank under the Directory, and the obloquy which pursued their names, were powerless to disturb them in their oblivion. Even their burial place was forgotten by an ungrateful posterity. 'The last resting place of patriots,' Saint-Just had ordained in his *Institutions Républicaines,* 'shall be set in a laughing country-side, and their graves covered with flowers to be sown each spring by the hands of children.'[2] But the bodies of the Robespierrists were buried in quicklime in the cemetery of Errancis, and the unmarked grave of these men of incorruptible virtue became later, by Fate's ironic commentary, the site of a public dance-hall.[2]

[1] Edmond Biré, *Journal d'un bourgeois de Paris pendant la terreur,* V, 402.
[2] O.C., II, 527.
[3] C. A. Dauban, *Paris en 1794 et en 1795* (Paris, 1869), p. 417; *L'Intermédiare de Chercheurs et Curieux,* XXIII, 714.

THE END

BIBLIOGRAPHICAL NOTE I

THE most useful collection of Saint-Just's writings is that edited by M. Charles Vellay under the title *Œuvres complètes de Saint-Just*, 2 volumes (Paris, 1908). Though it is not entirely above criticism, this edition easily supersedes all the earlier piecemeal collections, and is indispensable for the study of Saint-Just's life. It includes the *Discours sur les relations avec les puissances neutres* which there is now sufficient reason to believe Saint-Just did not write; and it omits some minor works, most of which M. Vellay has published elsewhere in various periodicals. The following list of these *lacunae* may be used to supplement the table of the *Œuvres complètes*.

'Fragments inédits de Saint-Just,' edited by Charles Vellay. *Revue politique et littéraire: Revue Bleue*, 5ᵉ série (1906), V, 353–58. This is a fragment of historical writing on the Château de Courcy.

'Œuvre inédite de Saint-Just: L'Arlequin Diogène,' edited by Charles Vellay, *Revue politique et littéraire: Revue Bleue*, 5ᵉ série, VIII (1907), 97–105.

'Une lettre inédite de Saint-Just,' edited by Charles Vellay, *Revue historique de la Révolution française*, IV (1913), 509–10.

'Une lettre de Saint-Just à Thullier,' edited by Charles Vellay, *Revue historique de la Révolution française*, I (1910), 101–02.

'Lettres inédites de Saint-Just,' edited by Charles Vellay, *Revue historique de la Révolution française*, I (1910), 481–92. Two of the letters from this series were reprinted in *Elsässische Monatschrift für Geschichte und Volkskunde*, II (1911), 410–13.

BIBLIOGRAPHICAL NOTE II

A BIBLIOGRAPHY of Saint-Just's published writings was compiled by M. Charles Vellay in 1910, and appeared, under the title 'Essai d'une bibliographie de Saint-Just,' in *La revue historique de la Révolution française*, I (1910), 418–35. The following year M. Vellay added some fifteen items to this list in a 'Complément à la bibliographie de Saint-Just,' published in the same journal, II (1911), 601–04. One new title and a few alternative editions which escaped M. Vellay's painstaking researches are noted below.

Discours sur le maximum de population des municipalités. Par St. Just. Imprimé par ordre de la Convention Nationale. Paris, 1793. 5 pp. in-8.

Rapport de St. Just au nom des Comités de salut public et de sûreté générale et décret de la Convention Nationale relatif aux personnes incarcérées. Du 8 Ventose, l'an 2 de la République Française une et indivisible. Imprimé par ordre de la Convention Nationale. 19 pp. A Poitiers, de l'Imprimerie de Barbier. N.D. [1794.]

Rapport sur les factions de l'étranger, et sur la conjuration ourdie par elles dans la République Française pour détruire le gouvernement républicain par la corruption et affamer Paris. Fait à la Convention Nationale le 23 ventose, l'an II de la République Française par St. Just au nom du Comité de salut public. Imprimé par ordre de la Convention Nationale. Paris, de l'Imprimerie nationale [1794], 20 pp.

Same. Another edition. De l'Imprimerie de la société des Jeunes Elèves de la Patrie dirigée par le citoyen Domergue. 26 pp. [Paris, 1794.]

Same. Another edition. De l'Imprimerie des Administrations Nationales. 28 pp. Paris [1794].

Same. Another edition. De l'Imprimerie Nationale. 26 pp. Paris [1794].

Rapport fait à la Convention Nationale au nom de ses comités de sûreté générale et de salut public sur la conjuration ourdie depuis plusieures années par les factions criminelles pour absorber la Révolution Française dans un changement de dynastie; et contre Fabre d'Eglantine, Danton, Philippeaux, Lacroix et Camille Desmoulins, prévenus de complicité dans ces Factions, et d'autres délits personnels contre la Liberté. Par Saint-Just. Séance du 11 germinal. Imprimé par ordre de la Convention Nationale. Imprimerie Nationale. Des Rédacteurs-Traducteurs des Séances de la Convention Nationale. 36 pp. Paris [1794].

   Same. Another edition. 24 pp.

   Same. Italian translation. 26 pp. In Parigi, nella Stamperia Nazionale Esecutiva del Louvre. An II [1794].

Notice des pièces authentiques relatives aux principaux agents de la faction de l'Etranger qui ont conspiré contre la souveraineté du peuple français et contre la représentation nationale. Imprimerie patriotique et républicaine, Paris, an II [1794]. 422 pp. (This pamphlet reprints Saint-Just's speeches in the Convention of March 13, 17, 31, and April 4, 1794.)

Œuvres politiques de Saint-Just. Discours et rapports recueillés et mis en ordre par H. Buffenoir. [2ᵉ éd.] Paris, 1895. 2 volumes. Collection A.-L. Guyot.

Organt, poème en vingt chants, par Saint-Just, avec la clef. 2 volumes of 134 and 138 pp., forming volumes 6 and 7 of the *Petite Bibliothèque de la curiosité érotique et galante.* This is a reimpression of the edition of 1789. Brussels, 1867.

LIST OF REFERENCES

Manuscript

Register of Baptisms, etc., Ville de Decize, Département de la Nièvre. The baptism of Louis Antoine de Saint-Just de Richebourg is recorded under date of August 25, 1767.
Bibliothèque Municipale de Nantes.
MS. 667,239. Letter of Saint-Just, dated July 13, 1793, concerning his report on the Girondists.
Archives Départementales du Nord, Lille.
MS. L 1238. Letter of Saint-Just written from Strasbourg, October 29, 1793. The address is lacking but the letter was probably addressed to Joseph Lebon at Arras.
Bibliothèque Municipale de Rouen.
Fonds Giradin — Autographes Nos. 802–04. Letter signed by Saint-Just and his fellow representatives Guyton and Gillet. Despatched from army headquarters at Marchienne au Pont to their colleagues Richard and Choudieu with the Army of the North, June 21, 1794.

Printed Works

Archives Parlementaires. Imprimé sous la direction de J. Mavidal et de E. Laurent. 1ᵉʳ série (1787–1799). Volumes I–LXXXII. Paris, 1879.
Aulard, François Victor Alphonse.
 Recueil des actes du Comité de salut public. 26 volumes. Paris, 1889–1923.
 Histoire de la Révolution Française. Paris, 1901.
 L'Eloquence parlementaire pendant la Révolution Française. 3 volumes. Paris, 1882–86.
 Etudes et Leçons sur la Révolution Française. 1ᵉʳ série. Paris, 1893.
 La Société des Jacobins. 6 volumes. Paris, 1889–97.
 'Les derniers instants de Couthon,' *La Révolution française,* XVIII (1897), 464–65.

Bapst, Germain.
'Inventaire des bibliothèques de quatre condamnés,' *La Révolution française*, XXI (1891), 532–36.
Barère de Vieuzac, Bertrand.
Mémoires. 4 volumes. Paris, 1842.
'Réponse de Barère, Billaud-Varennes, Collot d'Herbois et Vadier aux implications de Laurent Lecointre,' *La Révolution française*, XXXIV (1898), pp. 57–80, 154–77, 243–82.
Barras, Paul François Jean Nicholas, vicomte de.
Memoirs. Edited by George Duruy, translated by C. E. Roche. 4 volumes. New York, 1895–96.
Baudot, Marc-Antoine.
Notes historiques sur la Convention Nationale. Paris, 1893.
Bégis, Alfred.
'Saint-Just et les bureaux de Police Générale,' *Annuaire: Société des amis des livres*. Paris, 1896. Pp. 63–85.
Curiosités révolutionnaires. Saint-Just, membre du comité de salut public de la Convention Nationale, 1767–1794. Son emprisonnement sous Louis XVI en exécution d'une lettre de cachet. Paris, 1892.
Berty, A., and Legrand, H.
Histoire générale de Paris. Topographie historique du vieux Paris. 2 volumes. Paris, 1868.
Biré, Edmond.
Journal d'un bourgeois de Paris pendant la terreur. 5 volumes. Paris, 1895–1911.
Bonnal, Edmond.
Carnot. Paris, 1888.
Bonneral, F.
Cambon et la Révolution française. Paris, 1905.
Bruun, Geoffrey.
'Une traduction anglaise du faux rapport de Saint-Just rédigé par d'Antraigues.' *Annales historiques de la Révolution française*, N.S. IV (1927), 275–77.
'The Evolution of a Terrorist: Georges Auguste Couthon.' *Journal of Modern History*, II (1930), 410–29.
Buchez and Roux.
Histoire parlementaire de la Révolution française ou journal des assemblées nationales, 1789–1815. 40 vols. Paris, 1834–1838.

Bulletin historique et philologique des travaux historiques et scientifiques. Published by the Ministère de l'Instruction publique. Paris, 1902.

Carnot, Lazare.
Correspondance Générale. Edited by Etienne Charavay. 4 vols. Paris, 1892.

Carnot, Lazare Hippolyte.
Mémoires sur Carnot. Par son fils. 2 vols. Paris, 1861–63.

Charavay, Etienne.
'Le général Carlenc.' *Bulletin historique et philologique du comité des travaux historiques et scientifiques.* Paris, 1896, 523–54.

Chuquet, Arthur.
Les Guerres de la Révolution. 11 vols. Paris, 1888–96.

Courtois, Edmé Bonaventure.
Rapport... sur les évènemens du 9 thermidor. Paris, an IV [1796].

Coutant, B. (pseud. Stéfane-Pol).
'Autour de Robespierre: le conventionnel Le Bas.' *La Nouvelle Revue,* N.S. (1900), 77–106.

Dard, Emile.
Un épicurien sous la Terreur: Hérault de Séchelles (1759–1794). Paris, 1907.

Dauban, C. A.
Paris en 1794 et en 1795. Paris, 1869.

de Lacroix, J. P.
'Une lettre de Delacroix à Legendre.' *Annales révolutionnaires* XII (1920), 60–61.

Desmoulins, Camille.
Œuvres. 2 vols. Paris, 1836.
Réponse de Camille Desmoulins à Arthur Dillon. Paris, 1793.

Dommanget, Maurice.
'La famille de Saint-Just.' *Annales révolutionnaires,* VI (1913), 517–21.

d'Ornano, Cuneo.
Hoche, sa vie et correspondance. 2 vols. Paris, 1892.

d'Ossonville, Jean Baptiste.
'Fragments de mémoires de ——.' Edited by Charles Hericault. *La Revue de la Révolution,* III (1884), 1–21. Documents.

Fleury, Edmond.
 Saint-Just et la Terreur. 2 vols. Paris, 1852.
Fouché, Joseph.
 Memoirs. 2 vols. London, 1825.
Frénilly, François Auguste, Baron de.
 Recollections. Edited by Arthur Chuquet, translated by
  Frederic Lees. New York, 1909.
Gilbert, Nicolas Joseph Laurent.
 Œuvres. Edited by Charles Nodier. Paris, 1840.
Gosselin, Louis Léon Theodore (pseud. G. Lenôtre).
 Vieilles maisons, vieux papiers. 4 vols. Paris, 1900–10.
Hamel, Ernest.
 Histoire de Saint-Just. Paris, 1859.
 'Une épisode de la jeunesse de Saint-Just.' *La Révolution
  Française,* XXXII (1897), 97–120.
 'Saint-Just et Madame Thorin.' *La Révolution Française,*
  XXXII (1897), 348–363.
L'Intermédiare de Chercheurs et Curieux. Vol. XXII (1889), No.
  518 (December 10), pp. 714–15.
Jaurès, Jean.
 Histoire socialiste, 1789–1900. 12 vols. Paris, 1901–08.
Journal des débats et décrets. September, 1792, to Floréal, an V.
Journal de Physique. Vol. I. Paris, 1794.
Laurent, Gustave.
 'Le Faculté de Droit de Reims et les hommes de la Révolu-
  tion.' *Annales historiques de la Révolution Française,* XVII
  (1929), pp. 329–58.
Lecointre, Laurent.
 Robespierre peint par lui-même. Paris, 1794.
Levasseur, René.
 Mémoires. 4 vols. Paris, 1879.
Mathiez, Albert.
 'Une faux rapport de Saint-Just.' *Annales révolutionnaires.*
  VIII (1916), 599–611.
 La conspiration de l'étranger. Paris, 1918.
Méda, Charles André.
 *Précis historique des évènemens qui se sont passés dans la soirée
  du neuf thermidor, adressé au ministère de la guerre, le 30
  fructidor an X.* Paris, 1825. Baudoin Frères, Éditeurs.

Meillan, Arnaud.
Mémoires. Édited by Berville and Barrière. Paris, 1823.
Michon, Georges.
'La justice militaire sous la Révolution.' *Annales révolution-aires,* XIV (1922), 99–130.
Moniteur universal, ou Gazette nationale. 10 vols. 1789–1794.
Montier, Armand.
Robert Lindet. Paris, 1899.
Morsain, Antoine.
'Quelques antécédents de Saint-Just.' *Mercure de France,* LXV (1907), 193–210.
Paganel, M. P.
Essai historique et critique sur la révolution française. Paris, 1810.
Perroud, Claude.
La Proscription des Girondins. Paris, 1917.
Robespierre, Maximilian.
Discours et Rapports. Edited by Charles Vellay. Paris, 1908.
Papiers inédits trouvés chez Robespierre, Saint-Just, Payan, etc., supprimés ou omis par Courtois. 3 vols., Paris, 1828.
'Les notes de Robespierre contre les Dantonistes.' Edited by Albert Mathiez. *Annales révolutionnaires,* X (1918), 433–68.
Saint-Cyr, Gouvion.
Mémoires sur les campagnes des armées de Rhine. 4 vols. Paris, 1829.
Sainte Beuve, C. A. de.
Causeries de lundi. Troisième edition. V, 334–358. 'Saint-Just' (26 January, 1852).
Saint-Just, Louis Antoine de.
Œuvres complètes. Edited by Charles Vellay, 2 vols. Paris, 1908.
Thibaudeau, Antoine Claire, comte de.
Mémoires sur la Convention et la Directoire. Edited by Berville et Barrière. 2 vols. Paris, 1824.
Vatel, Charles.
Charlotte de Corday et les Girondins. 3 vols. Paris, 1864–72.
Vauthier, G.
'La succession de Saint-Just.' *Annales révolutionnaires,* XV (1923), 513–14.

Vellay, Charles.
  'Les poursuites contre l'Organt,' *Revue Bleue,* VIII (August 10,
    1907), No. 80, pp. 186–87.
  'Lettres inédites de Saint-Just,' *Revue historique de la Révolu-
    tion française,* I (1910), 101–02.
  'Une ami de Saint-Just: Gateau,' *Annales révolutionnaires,* I,
    (1908), 64–79.
Vidal, Gaston.
  Saint-Just. Paris, 1923.
Vilate, Joachim.
  Causes secrètes de la journée du 9 au 10 thermidor an 2. Edited
    by M. de Lescure. Paris, 1875.
Wallon, Henri.
  Histoire du Tribunal révolutionnaire de Paris. 6 vols. 1881.
  Les représentants du peuple. 5 vols. Paris, 1889.

                Some Later Studies on Saint-Just
Centore-Bineau, Denise B.
  Saint Just, 1767–1794. Paris, 1936.
Curtis, Eugene N.
  Saint-Just, colleague of Robespierre. New York, 1935.
Morton, John B.
  Saint-Just. London and New York, 1939.
Ollivier, Albert.
  Saint-Just et la forces des choses. Paris, 1955.

INDEX